THE ESSENTIAL

SEA KAYAKER

SECOND
EDITION

THE ESSENTIAL

SEA

KAYAKER

The Complete Guide for the Open-Water Paddler

SECOND EDITION

DAVID SEIDMAN

Illustrations by Andy Singer

Revised by Roseann Beggy Hanson
with Christopher Cunningham
and Jonathan Hanson, Technical Advisors

RAGGED MOUNTAIN PRESS / McGRAW-HILL

CAMDEN, MAINE • NEW YORK • SAN FRANCISCO • WASHINGTON, D.C. • AUCKLAND
BOGOTÁ • CARACAS • LISBON • LONDON • MADRID • MEXICO CITY • MILAN
MONTREAL • NEW DELHI • SAN JUAN • SINGAPORE • SYDNEY • TOKYO • TORONTO

ALSO IN THE RAGGED MOUNTAIN PRESS ESSENTIAL SERIES
The Essential Backpacker: A Complete Guide for the Foot Traveler, Adrienne Hall
The Essential Cross-Country Skier: A Step-by-Step Guide, Paul Petersen and Richard A. Lovett
The Essential Outdoor Gear Manual: Equipment Care, Repair, and Selection, 2nd edition,
    Annie Getchell and Dave Getchell Jr.
The Essential Touring Cyclist: A Complete Guide for the Bicycle Traveler, 2nd edition, Richard A. Lovett
The Essential Snowshoer: A Step-by-Step Guide, Marianne Zwosta
The Essential Whitewater Kayaker: A Complete Course, Jeff Bennett
The Essential Wilderness Navigator, 2nd edition, David Seidman and Paul Cleveland

Ragged Mountain Press
A Division of The McGraw·Hill Companies

10 9 8 7 6 5 4 3
Copyright © 1992, 2001 Ragged Mountain Press
All rights reserved. The publisher takes no responsibility for the use of any of the materials or
methods described in this book, nor for the products thereof. The name "Ragged Mountain Press"
and the Ragged Mountain Press logo are trademarks of The McGraw-Hill Companies. Printed in
the United States of America.

Library of Congress Cataloging-in-Publication Data
Seidman, David.
    The essential sea kayaker : a complete course for the open-water paddler / David
    Seidman ; illustrations by Andy Singer ; revised by Roseann Beggy Hanson ; with
    Christopher Cunningham and Jonathan Hanson, technical advisors.—2nd ed.
        p.   cm.
    Includes bibliographical references (p.   ) and index.
    ISBN 0-07-136237-1
    1. Sea Kayaking.   I. Hanson, Roseann Beggy.   II. Title.
GV788.5.S45 2001
797.1'224—dc21   00-042184

Questions regarding the content of this book should be addressed to
Ragged Mountain Press
P.O. Box 220
Camden, ME 04843
www.raggedmountainpress.com

Questions regarding the ordering of this book should be addressed to
The McGraw-Hill Companies
Customer Service Department
P.O. Box 547
Blacklick, OH 43004
Retail customers: 1-800-262-4729
Bookstores: 1-800-722-4726

This book is printed on 70 lb. Citation at R. R. Donnelley & Sons, Crawfordsville, IN
Design by Dede Cummings
Production by PerfecType and Dan Kirchoff
Edited by Tom McCarthy and Larry Floersch
All photos courtesy David Seidman unless otherwise noted.
Bonine, Dacron, Freshette, Gore-Tex, Kevlar, Lycra, Shake 'n Bake, Snickers, Snoopy, and Velcro are
registered trademarks.

WARNING: Sea kayaking can take paddlers into harm's way, exposing them to risks of injury, cold-
water exposure and hypothermia, drowning, and other hazards that can lead to serious injury or death.
   This book is not intended to replace instruction by a qualified teacher or to substitute for good personal
judgment. In using this book, the reader releases the author, publisher, and distributor from liability for any
loss or injury, including death, allegedly caused, in whole or in part, by relying on information contained in this book.

To Andy,
who showed me the ropes;
and Laura,
who showed me how to untie them.

On Seamanship

thoughts for those who go to sea in small craft

One of the paradoxes of sea kayaking is the ease with which one can acquire the physical skills required. In just two or three days a person of average balance and dexterity, and with a good coach, can master a relatively advanced level of skills, including kayaking turns, braces, and a roll. But as with any form of boating on the sea, this is only the beginning. Because the kayak has an average speed of barely three knots, it is particularly susceptible to the vagaries of currents and wind. Although its shallow draft and light weight mean it can negotiate surf beaches and rocky shores not attempted by other craft, these characteristics render it vulnerable to wind and strong current. It is important that, once the physical skills have been acquired, the many lessons of kayak seamanship begin.

As is true of every way of going on the sea, in big ships or in small kayaks, the disciplines of seamanship—the judgment, the knowledge of the vessel and all its parts, the weather sensibility, and the prudent awareness of one's own skills and strengths—usually take years of learning and constant reinforcement. Sound judgment, as is so often the case with such things, is usually more obvious by its absence than its presence. It is also a beast whose image fades with familiarity and changing circumstance. Fatigue will diminish it and conflicting desires and requirements become the medium for its expression—or lack thereof.

As a beginner, or one of long experience, it is very easy then to miss the whole point, the key ingredient that holds the whole mass together; lose your humility for the sea and the whole thing falls apart.

Go with respect, and live to enjoy.

—John Dowd
Kayak Voyager

CONTENTS

PREFACE TO THE SECOND EDITION

Sea kayaking is no longer just for the hard-core adventurer. In the eight years since the readers of the first edition of *The Essential Sea Kayaker* snapped on spray skirts, picked up paddles, and headed out, the sport has opened up to the world. Nowadays it's rare to visit any body of water bigger than a pond and not see kayakers of all types paddling away. Times have changed, and so has this book.

For nearly a decade the first edition was a best-seller and trusted companion for novice sea kayakers. It was used by schools, recommended to friends, and praised by kayakers more knowledgeable than I'll ever be. The book attracted attention because it was the first to distill the basics, clearly and simply—introducing tens of thousands of new paddlers to the joys of kayaking. Through luck or skill I must have gotten it right, because it's taken the better part of a decade for someone to suggest a second edition. So here it is, with only a few changes to the basics and a lot of useful new stuff added on. And that's good, since that's also what sea kayaking is about: the basics stay the same while you keep adding on and learning more.

Back when I was learning to paddle, the only books around were by opinionated, die-hard experts. Great if you wanted to launch an expedition to Greenland, but I just wanted to have some fun—which is why I wrote the first edition. It was meant for someone like myself (or you), who was just getting started. The idea was to make it easy and enjoyable, like the sport of sea kayaking (as long as you avoid Greenland).

This second edition is still written so you can have fun, only more of it. When you're ready to head out beyond the shelter of your favorite cove, you'll find information on navigation and how to deal with wind, weather, fog, tides, currents, boat traffic, and paddling at night. I've included ways to take care of your body with warm-up techniques, and how to avoid things like seasickness, hypothermia, and tendonitis. At the end there's an expanded resource section for disabled paddlers and families, and suggestions for further reading and lists of manufacturers.

So get out there, give it a try, and hopefully we'll both be paddling around in the next decade when I add on some more for the third edition.

David Seidman
January 2001

INTRODUCTION

MY PROMISE TO YOU

This book will give you the essence, the techniques, and the specifics of the sport of sea kayaking. With that knowledge you'll be able to acquire the skills that will make sea kayaking the rewarding and enjoyable sport it should be. It will also get you thinking about long cruises in the Bahamas or getting better aerobic exercise out of an evening's paddle. Sound like what you're looking for? Good, because in the following pages you'll find a place to start and a place to which you can return as you continue to develop. It'll be easy. I promise.

KNOW YOUR AUTHOR

When I embarked on writing a sea kayaking book for beginners, I decided to go out and find an expert, learn from him, and then tell you about it in a way that would make sense. The words in this book are mine, speaking to you as the consummate klutz . . . I hope you are much less of one. Most of the substance has been supplied by Andy Singer.

Andy is a rare find, yet in some ways he's typical of the people involved in sea kayaking. He owns a company whose purported business is to design, build, and sell kayaks. Does he sell many? Not really. He's too busy paddling, something he's been doing since the 1960s; he took up teaching in the early 1980s. He's patient and inventive, and learning from him is fun. Whatever I've learned I've gotten from him, which must mean something because I'm still here to write about it.

For the rest of this book you will be Andy's student, too. Since you can't really be there with him, I'll be there for you. I'll make the goofs, ask the dumb questions, and then explain it to you. Included in this edition revised and expanded by Roseann Beggy Hanson are the expertise and advice of sea kayaking experts Chris Cunningham, editor of *Sea Kayaker* magazine, and Jonathan Hanson, a veteran sea kayak tourer. All you'll have to do is read, think, and practice.

HOW TO USE THIS BOOK

I've laid things out in a progressive format, from beginner's courses to advanced techniques. You start here, go there next, and then finally wind up where you want to be. Once you've learned something, you'll use it to learn something else. As ideas accumulate, you'll be surprised how far you've progressed.

Remember that this or any other book on sea kayaking is worthless unless you get out on the water and try what you've been reading about. Read, yes. Study, yes. Listen to other paddlers, sure. But your time on the water and the mistakes you make will give you the best education.

So get out there, get wet, have fun, and do it!

TEN MOST FREQUENTLY ASKED QUESTIONS

1. Don't Kayaks Tip Over?

Yes, sea kayaks can tip over—in fact, they are designed to do so. But before you give up and buy a cabin cruiser, read on.

The sea kayaks we paddle today are the product of more than 5,000 years of evolution. Coastal people of the Arctic built these craft to deal with the unique problems of their environment, and groups separated by thousands of miles produced what was essentially the same answer, which is a good indication that what they came up with was sound.

A sea kayak is long and narrow, compared to the stubbier river kayak, and has a closed deck and a cockpit sealed with a fabric skirt, which makes it nearly watertight. Its low profile, compared to high-sided canoes or larger craft, reduces its susceptibility to wind and waves. Powered by a double-bladed paddle, it is responsive and easy to balance under even extreme conditions. When capsized, it can be rolled upright with a minimum of effort, making it, in effect, as self-righting as a lifeboat. The end result is one of the safest deepwater vessels ever created, a vessel that supported large cultures for thousands of years.

Part 2 of this book, Sea Kayaking 102: Heading Out, teaches you all about rolling and self-rescues.

2. If It Goes Over, Will I Be Trapped?

It is quite likely that you will be able to exit your sea kayak if you capsize and cannot roll back up. It is also possible to remain in your capsized boat and twist your torso and head to the surface and breathe, so don't panic about getting stuck underwater in your boat.

Part 1, Sea Kayaking 101, gives you the skills and confidence you need to get in—and out—of your boat when you need to.

3. How Do I Steer the Thing?

Your paddle does the steering. Plus most sea kayaks today also have a built-in rudder that is controlled by thin cables attached to foot controls; you push on the left pedal to turn left and vice-versa. Another direction-control option is a skeg (more common on English boats). A skeg is a retractable fin mounted on the bottom of the hull, and it mostly helps keep the kayak moving in a straight line.

In Sea Kayaking 101, the Paddling Basics chapter goes into all the techniques of paddle strokes for controlling your boat expertly and effortlessly.

4. How Can I Carry Such a Big Boat by Myself?

Although sea kayaks, at about 15 to 20 feet long and 40 to 50 pounds, seem like impossibly unwieldy packages to lug around, it's not as hard as you'd think. There are tricks for shouldering and walking with a boat as well as clever accessories such as strap-on wheels for long hauls. This is covered in the Meet Your Kayak chapter in Sea Kayaking 101.

5. Do I Need to Know a Lot about Seamanship to Paddle on Open Water?

The term *sea kayaking* might be a bit misleading. It is rarely done on the open sea; most folks prefer to just putter along the coastlines of bays, lakes, and creeks, watching the scenery. However, although you don't need to go out and get a coast guard license to safely voyage in a sea kayak, you should learn the basics of waves, weather, and navigation. In part 3 of this book, Graduate Courses, the chapter Sea and Sky will get you started in the right direction.

6. Why Do Most Books Make Sea Kayaking Sound Like a Dangerous Survival Sport?

Sea kayaking is like any outdoor activity: it has its risks. A few kayaking authorities-cum-authors are pretty gonzo and enjoy emphasizing the thrilling—and dangerous—aspects of exploring the sea in a small, self-powered craft. Other authors feel they are doing you a service in counseling you that you can get hurt or die sea kayaking, just as you can when climbing or mountaineering or even hiking. The best insurance you have against getting hurt is

JONATHAN HANSON

education and experience. So read, practice, and don't worry.

7. What If I Don't Have Arms like Arnold Schwarzenegger?

As in rock climbing, success in sea kayaking has more to do with technique than brawn, which you'll learn about in Paddling Basics. Finesse triumphs over strength. Having the right gear and being in reasonably good cardiovascular shape are also important. Certainly neither your age nor your sex has anything to do with successful kayaking. Eskimos encouraged their children to play in kayaks from about 5 years on, and by age 12 they were learning to roll upright from an inverted position. Kids around 8 or 9 years of age have a remarkable sense of balance and movement, and do surprisingly well compared with adult novices. Seniors should not be scared off either. The kayak's seated position is comfortable and supportive, and the exercise of paddling can be as strenuous or leisurely as you like, perfect for low-impact upper body and aerobic exercise. And today there are many physically challenged kayakers plying the waters of the world.

8. How Far Can I Go?

With efficient, smooth paddling technique and gear that fits you right, you can paddle a surprising distance in a leisurely day—20 or more miles seems like nothing in calm conditions, as you take in all the wonderful sights and sounds

9. Am I Going to Have to Buy Tons of Gear?

The basic kit of a kayaker is pretty simple: boat, paddle and spare, spray skirt, life jacket, and a few safety items such as flares, a bailing device, and a paddle float. You can get started with all-new gear, or you can buy a used boat and mix old and new accessories and keep your investment to a minimum. If you're lucky to live near a full-service kayak store, you can rent a boat for a while before deciding to take the plunge.

Chances are if you hike or ride a bike, you already own much of the clothing you'll need: synthetic tops and bottoms, fleece midlayers, waterproof shell. Shorts and a T-shirt are OK for learning and paddling if you're just a few feet off shore, but for any extended day-or-longer excursions, you should be dressed for the water temperature in case of capsize and extended time spent floating in the water.

The basic gear for backpacking—tent, stove, sleeping bag—is perfect for kayak camping. All you'll need are waterproof bags for stowage.

How to choose the right stuff is explained in the What You Will Need chapter, in Sea Kayaking 101

10. Where Do I Find Out More?

Today there are thousands of resources for paddlers, from friendly full-service hometown shops to sites on the Internet, as well as hundreds of clubs and schools and tour companies. The paddler's resources at the end of this book will be your launch pad for more explorations into the world of sea kayaking.

SETTING FORTH

The first part of this course, SK 101, is not just for beginners. Although it is a place to start, it is also a place to which you should return. If you are just beginning, it is here that you'll develop traits that will stand you in good stead for the rest of your paddling days. If you have sea time already, this section will be a good way to check your technique and refine what you already know.

It has been said that the person claiming ten years' experience is likely to be someone with one year of learning and nine years of repeating the same things. So don't feel ashamed about coming back to make sure you've gotten the fundamentals down pat.

In SK 101 you'll gather the equipment you'll need, learn to use it, get moving, and sample things to come.

If you're new to sea kayaking, follow the sections in the order presented. The book has been designed to build on experience. Read one complete section and then stop. Get a good overview of the principles behind it. Then go out and tackle that section one step at a time. Work on it until you feel comfortable with what you are doing. If in doubt, and you can't find an experienced guide, have someone else read and go over the step that troubles you. Even though that person might not understand sea kayaking, he or she will at least bring an objective point of view to the problem.

There are no great mysteries to the basic techniques of sea kayaking. Just keep trying and eventually you'll get them. But you're going to have to work at it in the beginning, so don't feel discouraged if things don't flow at first.

Don't pressure yourself either. Sea kayaking is not a competitive pastime. Someday your only challenger will be the open water, and it couldn't care less. But for now, in the beginning, it's only your ego. So back off, go easy on yourself, and enjoy the learning. If you feel that you're not getting the hang of one step, go on to the others in that section. Work around it, while periodically coming back to it. Eventually, and not too far in the future, it will all come together.

There are paddlers out there who taught themselves. If you're one of these people, you might be tempted to look through SK 101 and think that it's not for you. But it is. Even though you might be able to perform all of the maneuvers, there is more often than not one small but key ingredient you've missed: something that will make your life easier, your paddling less strenuous, or your trips a little safer. As with many of us, you might be substituting strength and luck for the ultimate reliability of a perfected style.

Remember: overconfidence, and the false sense of security that comes with it, have created more frightening situations for sea kayakers than anything else. The only way to know your limits is to know yourself. And the only way to know yourself is to gauge your ability against a set of standards. This book provides those standards.

WHAT YOU WILL NEED

1

KAYAK

First we should come to an agreement on the definition of a sea kayak. You could, of course, go to sea in almost any kind of kayak, but a more realistic approach would be to have a boat that maximizes your safety, comfort, efficiency, and enjoyment.

Because it will spend most of its time on a straight course rather than twisting around rocks in a river, a sea kayak needs to be directionally stable. That is, it should not force the paddler to work at keeping it going in a straight line. Because a sea kayak depends on the paddler for all of its forward momentum, it should require only a minimum of effort to achieve and maintain a fast cruising speed. Because you will probably spend long periods in the kayak, it must offer an acceptable level of creature comfort. It should also provide another type of comfort related to handling the waters it is sent out to meet. This comfort is known as *seaworthiness* and is the ultimate test of the sea kayak's abilities.

As you can see, the boat described is job-specific. It will be good for one thing and that one only. It would be hopelessly awkward on narrow rivers and almost useless in whitewater. But if your goal is to venture onto open waters, put many miles under your keel, or poke your bow around the next headland, then the boat defined as a sea kayak is right for you.

Now that we have a generic definition, we can explore the more specific aspects of your personal sea kayak. For it is here that we can start narrowing the field to help you find the boat that will best fit your needs. It is also here that beginners may go a little crazy. And rightfully so. How do you pick the proper kayak when you have no basis for your choice? The answer is you don't. And that's OK.

If you listen to every expert you'll never come to a decision. Your best option is to get as close as you can to a general-purpose touring sea kayak (15 to 17 feet long, 23 to 25 inches wide, and of moderate carrying capacity) with a good resale value. Starting with a middle-of-the-road design, and the philosophy that your first boat isn't going to have to last you the rest of your life, will make things a lot easier.

Don't be afraid to go by your instincts. As much as you can with anything new, make sure that your first boat feels right, not awkward or threatening. Try as many boats as you can in the water, then buy the one in which you feel the most relaxed and that is most appealing to your eye (kayaking is personal stuff, and looks definitely count). If it feels and looks right, you'll use it. And the more you use it, the faster you'll learn. As you gain experience, your ideas about the right boat will change, sometimes dramatically. Every chance you get, rent or borrow other kayaks and try them.

A good place to start may be with any of the polyethylene plastic kayaks made by the larger manufacturers. There is nothing extreme in their designs, they have all the basic features, are almost indestructible, paddle reasonably well, and maintain a good resale value. They are also comparatively inexpensive. So if you find that sea kayaking is not for you, you haven't made a large investment in something that is going to wind up as a planter in your backyard. If these boats don't appeal to you, consider any of the fiberglass kayaks that may be popular in your area.

Once you do have a realistic understanding of your requirements, the act of choosing a kayak becomes the single most important step in directing your involvement in the sport. The boat you pick will affect your choice of paddle, paddling style, accessories, and psychological attitude. Sound intimidating? Well, don't worry. Remember: No one has yet found the perfect kayak. And if anyone did, he or she would probably try to improve it somehow.

The first question in choosing a kayak is, "How do you envision using it?" If the idea of long expeditions into the wilderness attracts you, you'll want something with a lot of space for stowage. This will probably necessitate a moderately broad beam. Keep in mind, however, that the broader the boat, the slower it will be, and for long days on the water this will be tiring, so you will want to compromise between high volume and fast hull shape. Most kayak manufacturers produce at least one model with touring in mind, so be sure to ask your salesperson to show you these. It will also have to be rugged and therefore is likely to be heavy, although many manufacturers today use high-tech materials that are both strong and light (and expensive). If you

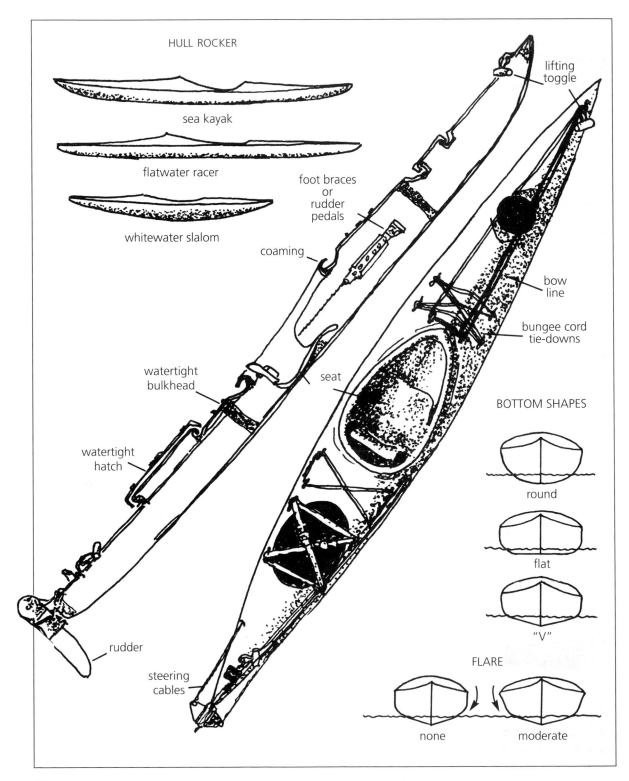

HULL ROCKER

sea kayak

flatwater racer

whitewater slalom

lifting toggle

foot braces or rudder pedals

coaming

bow line

bungee cord tie-downs

watertight bulkhead

seat

watertight hatch

BOTTOM SHAPES

round

flat

"V"

rudder

steering cables

FLARE

moderate

think you'll be heading cross-country or overseas to paddle, a folding kayak that comes apart for easier shipping could be handy.

For nature watching or fishing you'll want a very stable kayak that can be left to its own devices while you deal with equipment or fish; think broad beam here. It would also be advantageous to have a boat that could turn quickly or within a limited space.

If you're just interested in short day trips, and almost 40 percent of all sea kayakers are, you'll want a boat that can reach its best speed with a minimum of effort. It should be something lively and fast that will give you an invigorating workout and challenge your abilities.

Once you've decided how you will use the boat, you have to start thinking about which type of kayak will do the best job. Ask yourself what trade-offs you are willing to make to satisfy your goals. Here are some choices and the compromises that go with them.

Single or Double?

If you will always be paddling with someone else, then it is worth considering a double, a kayak for two paddlers. Doubles are ideal if you and your partner are of significantly different strengths or abilities. Doubles also cost about a third less than two singles, are theoretically faster because of their longer length, are more stable, and often are more comfortable in rough seas. On the other hand, a double is not as responsive as a single, it has less stowage than two singles, it offers less personal freedom, and it cannot be easily paddled by one person.

Slow and Stable or Fast and Tippy?

Here are a few guidelines regarding performance.

Wide boats are generally slower but are more sta-ble than narrow ones. Less force is required to move narrow boats than wide boats. The longer the water-line length (i.e., the length of the hull that is actually in the water, not the overall hull length from bow to stern), the higher a boat's potential top speed.

Flat-bottomed boats are steady when upright, with stability increasing rapidly as the boat leans (heels) to a specific angle, after which they can capsize abruptly. V-bottomed boats are less steady in the upright position, with stability increasing as they are heeled over; the capsizing point is reached gradually. Round-bottomed boats are the least steady of all, with stability being the same when upright as when tilted. A round bottom is also the shape with the least resistance, presenting the minimum amount of wetted surface area for a given volume. Adding flare to the sides of any of these hull shapes increases their stability at extreme angles. Most sea kayaks have gently rounded hulls that incorporate a little of each bottom type and flare (see illustration, left).

Speed and maneuverability are incompatible. The more curve (rocker) in a boat's bottom as seen in profile lengthwise, the slower the boat, but the easier it will be to turn. For example, a flatwater racer, which has slight to moderate rocker, can be moved through the water with minimal effort but is difficult to turn. The opposite is true of a highly rockered whitewater slalom kayak. A touring sea kayak is somewhere in between.

Real-world speed differences between kayaks are not all that great. Most can be paddled at 3 knots easily, with short spurts to 4 or 5 knots. A boat might have a 6-knot potential, but few recreational paddlers could get it there. More important than ultimate speed is the ease with which you can move the boat.

For those who are more athletic and adventuresome, a swift yet responsive ("tippy") boat will be best. You can go farther and faster for a given energy output, but you pay in reduced stability.

Two singles or one double? Be sure to try out both options if you're a paddling couple. Well-suited couples on dry land may face difficulties with a one-kayak partnership.

For those who are more conservative, a stable boat will be best. You will have to work harder to keep it going, but to some degree it will look after itself when you can't, and it will place fewer demands on your capabilities as a paddler.

There are boats that compromise and try to give you a little of each, or none of either, depending on how you look at it.

Rigid or Collapsible?

The only reason not to purchase a rigid boat is if you intend to take it with you on an airplane or your only storage facility is a closet.

Collapsible boats can either be take-apart or folding. Take-apart kayaks are usually standard fiberglass models that have been sectionalized. They are not as easy to store, are more expensive, and are more vulnerable to damage in shipping than folding ones, but their carrying capacity and performance are usually superior.

With a folding boat, a canvas-like skin is stretched over an assembled wood or aluminum frame; the boat can be stowed in one to three bags. Folding boats tend to be wider, slower, quieter, and more stable than rigid kayaks. They have also proved to be extremely seaworthy, and many designs today provide surprisingly good performance. Folding kayaks are more expensive and require considerably more care than hardshell boats in their use and upkeep. Although assembly averages only 20 minutes and disassembly a little longer, this could become a tedious chore if done on a regular basis.

For rigid construction, probably the best material to date is fiberglass. It can be made strong, flexible, and light, with the average single fiberglass kayak weighing 55 pounds. Kevlar can be incorporated into fiberglass construction to reduce weight, while simultaneously retaining strength and increasing cost.

Roto-molded, polyethylene plastic construction is stronger and 25 percent less expensive, but about 10 percent heavier, than fiberglass. Plastic is placed in a sealed, heated mold that is rotated. When the melted plastic cools, you have a one-piece kayak. These boats are almost indestructible but can be deformed by heat or uneven pressure if stored or transported improperly. Fairly new on the boat scene is polycarbonate, which is a step up from polyethylene in price and produces a more rigid, smoother hull that is less susceptible to degradation by ultraviolet light and gouging.

Meeting Your Standards

Once you have narrowed your choice to a type of sea kayak, you have to judge if the specific boat you've chosen meets your standards.

- Are you and your boat a good fit? All kayaks require internal adjustments, but the fit should at least be close. Take into consideration if there is enough foot room and support or contact points for your knees, thighs, hips, rear, and lower back. Sit in it for a while before passing judgment. Never buy a boat without trying it on.
- Is there enough stability to make you feel secure? Does its stability feel predictable, or does it become suddenly unstable if leaned too far?
- Is it easy to paddle? A good way to judge this is by paddling into a headwind and waves.
- How difficult is it to turn or to paddle in a straight line? How does it want to point in relation to the wind when still and when underway?
- Do you like its looks? You'll be spending a lot of time with it, so you might as well like the way it looks. Color is important, too. Yellow is the most visible, white shows the least wear, and deep blues and red fade the fastest.
- Can you lift and carry it by yourself? Would it be too difficult to hoist on a car rack?
- Is there enough reserve buoyancy in the form of airbags or watertight bulkheads to float you and the boat when it is swamped?
- Are there fittings such as lifting toggles, a bow line for towing, deck bungee cords, and good watertight hatches? Are they strong and up to the job?
- Does it need and have a skeg or rudder?
- Can it hold all your gear without your having to lash any on deck?
- Is it well-built? Only a professional can really judge this, but there are clues. Check the finish both inside and out. See how things fit, especially in hidden areas. If the builder cared about the details, a similar attitude was probably applied to the rest of the construction.
- Price? An expensive boat is not always a good boat; but an inexpensive one rarely is. Remember: quality costs initially but pays off in the long run.

PADDLE

The double-bladed paddle is used to propel, steer, and provide a stabilizing force for the boat. It works as part of an integrated system that also includes the kayak and your body. All three components interlock and affect each other in a way that is infinitely variable. This is why choosing the right paddle is so important, yet at the same time so difficult and subjective.

The paddle works as a variable lever that, through the movable fulcrum supplied by your lower hand, digs into the water so you can pull the kayak toward and past it. Through careful choices you can make sure that this lever matches your capabilities so that you avoid putting undue strain on tendons and muscles, while still providing the necessary thrust for the hull in which you are sitting. Balance is the key.

Materials

You can take a step toward achieving this balance by using the lightest paddle possible. Naturally you won't want to forfeit strength to do this. To get both strength and lightness takes money, but it will be money well spent, and the investment will look better with each hour you spend holding the paddle. Average paddles weigh 2½ pounds. A paddle over 3 pounds is too heavy and one under 2 pounds is in the domain of costly, high-tech materials.

The best paddle for general service has a fiberglass shaft and blade. Fiberglass is strong, light, and has some spring to it. Exotic cores or reinforcements (such as carbon fiber, graphite, or Kevlar) can be incorporated into a fiberglass paddle to reduce weight without sacrificing strength—for a price. A well-made, laminated wood paddle is still a desirable standard. Without a doubt the worst is an aluminum shaft with plastic blades. It will be cold to the touch, heavy, poorly balanced, and usually ill-formed, but it will be cheap.

Remember you will be buying two paddles: a primary and a spare. Don't go ultracheap on the spare, because the conditions in which you are likely to break or lose your primary paddle will be nasty—not the place to have a cheap paddle.

Length

The next step is to ascertain the proper paddle length and blade type for your personal style, which is a combination of the pace and force with which you feel most comfortable under most circumstances. Take care in this choice; the wrong length or blade shape can cause a lot of body strain.

Your boat and how you sit in it are the first factors to consider. If your seated position is low in the kayak, or if the kayak is wide, you will need a longer paddle to reach the water. The opposite is true if you sit tall or have a narrower boat.

Your preference for a particular pace is also important. All other things being equal, longer paddles require a slower stroke with a lot more power behind them than shorter paddles. The energy output will be the same for both, but only one (or something in between) will feel comfortable for you and your particular kayak. Try a variety of paddles from 7 to 8½ feet long, all with the same blade shape. Paddle into a moderate headwind for about 15 minutes with each. You'll know right off which feels most comfortable.

Blade

Blades also will influence your style of paddling. Blades with a lot of area or a shape that grips the water (such as a curved blade), require a lot of power behind them and will also be affected by wind. Blades with less area or a slippery shape (such as a narrow blade), require less power and are less affected on windy days.

Don't be fooled by blades that seem to slip. They are not wasting energy. It may take longer to accelerate a boat with them, but you can keep it going at a constant rate with a lot less effort and impact on your body. By comparison, you can accelerate a boat faster with blades that seem to dig in, which will help in making turns or when using the paddle to provide an upward force to enhance stability. Both types of blades work when used for their intended job.

For example, the traditional long and narrow shape of an Eskimo blade was dictated by the fact that the user had to paddle great distances at a steady speed over open water. Bursts of power were rare. At the other extreme is the modern paddler in whitewater or surf, who needs a wide blade with its more immediate grip on the water for sudden applications of power to move, steer, or right the boat. Both are working as efficient levers.

To select the best blade for you and your boat,

test paddles of the same length but different blade types by paddling into the wind for at least 15 minutes with each type. Also try bracing strokes to find which blades give you an acceptable amount of support.

A blade that is asymmetrical is a definite asset (see illustration, right). When a paddle is drawn through the water by the kayaker, the shaft, and therefore the blade, are slanted 40 degrees or so to the surface of the water rather than straight up-and-down. An asymmetrical blade adds more area to the outside edge so that when it is placed in the water at a natural paddling angle, more of the blade is drawn through the water than if the blade were symmetrical. Therefore, the kayaker gets more power.

No one paddle length, blade type, or combination thereof will be right for all conditions. Wind strength, sea state, your experience, and your varying levels of energy will all be factors. Intelligent compromise is the best we can hope for. This may seem a daunting and somewhat cavalier proposal. Find a comfortable paddle length as described here, using a blade that is either flat or only mildly curved. This type of blade will often be less expensive and is easier to orient with respect to the water in different movements. Another option is to find your optimum length, and then buy one paddle of each blade shape (narrow and wide), one for the primary and one for a spare; then you can switch off as conditions warrant.

Feathered or Nonfeathered

When selecting a paddle you will also have to decide whether it is to be feathered or nonfeathered. A feathered paddle has its blades offset 60 to 90 degrees from each other; the paddle is designated as either right- or left-hand controlled, depending on how the power (concave) faces of the blades are oriented. A nonfeathered paddle has both blades in the same plane. Rather than buying three paddles to find which style you like best, buy one take-apart paddle that can be set to all three positions (nonfeathered, right-hand feathered, and left-hand feathered). This will let you experiment and give you a good on-board spare paddle once you have decided which one you prefer. When purchasing a

take-apart paddle, inspect the connecting joint, known as the ferrule, for strength and a minimum amount of play.

Neither feathering nor nonfeathering is superior, and both have their advocates and detractors. Feathering is thought to provide a slight mechanical advantage and to offer less wind resistance on the airborne blade when you are paddling into the wind. Nonfeathering may reduce stress on wrist muscles and offers less resistance on the airborne blade when you are paddling with the wind on your side. Both techniques will be thoroughly reviewed in the section about paddling.

To determine the configuration of your paddle, stand it in front of you with the lower blade's power face pointing toward you. If the upper blade's power face points to your left, it is a left-hand-controlled feathered paddle; if it is to your right, it is a right-hand-controlled feathered paddle; if both blades face the same direction, it is a nonfeathered paddle. A feathered paddle with flat blades can be either right- or left-handed, because flat blades have no set power faces.

Remember: the best paddle is the one that feels most comfortable when the wind and waves kick up.

Shaft

Beyond the basics, there are some niceties to look for in a paddle. A shaft that is oval in cross section where it is held by the controlling hand might be advantageous. This shape gives a better grip because of the way we grasp objects. It also is used to keep the blades properly aligned to your hand and the water. However, an oval shaft may be restrictive to some paddlers who like to alter blade angle to suit their stroke without twisting their wrists into awkward positions. For them a round shaft is best.

To improve your grip, keep the shaft dry by using drip rings. Your grip on a wooden shaft can also be improved by lightly sanding the shaft where it is held by the controlling hand with #400 sandpaper or steel wool. Fiberglass shafts must be sanded gently in order to avoid raising glass fibers, which can be very irritating. An alternative to sanding is to place a section of bicycle inner tube or the tape used on tennis racquet handles over the shaft.

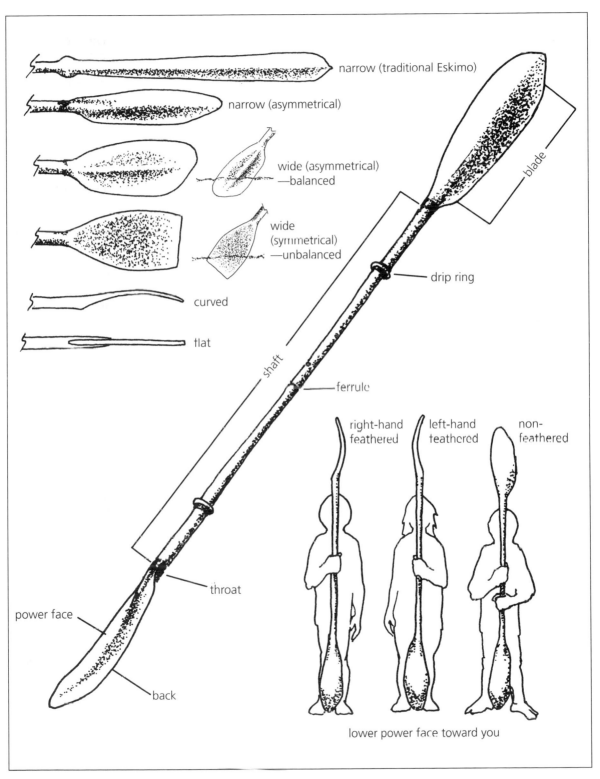

narrow (traditional Eskimo)

narrow (asymmetrical)

wide (asymmetrical) —balanced

wide (symmetrical) —unbalanced

curved

flat

blade

drip ring

shaft

ferrule

right-hand feathered

left-hand feathered

non-feathered

throat

power face

back

lower power face toward you

23

GEAR

Spray Skirt

It is ironic that the one item that gives a kayak its ultimate seaworthiness is also the one that most frightens people. Spray skirts seal out water and make a kayak reliably buoyant. So don't worry, a properly fitted spray skirt will not trap you in your boat. Once you begin to feel more at home in your kayak, the act of snapping the spray skirt in place brings with it a certain sense of security. It will keep your legs and lower body dry and warm, and you and the boat safe.

A spray skirt is like a waterproof ballerina's tutu. You step into it and pull it up so the skirt part flares out at your waist. The upper part, called a *chimney* or *tunnel*, should come to just under your armpits, but not so high that it chafes or is uncomfortable.

If you plan to paddle in rough water, choose a neoprene spray skirt. When stretched around the coaming, it makes a taut deck that easily sheds water, and the tunnel fits snugly around the torso, making a flexible yet waterproof closure. Because of its snug fit, this type of spray skirt often comes in sizes: one size for the skirt, so it will fit the coaming of your boat; and another size for the tunnel, so it will fit you. A properly fitting skirt should not have to be stretched more than ½ inch on all sides to make a good seal with the cockpit's coaming. The tunnel is usually marked for your waist size and should be 85 percent of that measurement when unstretched.

Tight neoprene skirts can chafe or can be too hot on long tours, especially in warm climates. An alternative to the neoprene spray skirt is one made of coated nylon. These are lighter, less expensive, and cooler in warm weather, but the waterproofing will eventually break down or wear as it rubs against the coaming. Cheap nylon skirts do not create as taut a deck as a neoprene skirt; they tend to sag, which allows water to puddle. Also, nylon tunnels will not fit as snugly or stay up as easily. For those who like the lightness of nylon but don't want to put up with its drawbacks, there are spray skirts made of neoprene but with a nylon tunnel. If built well, these can be a comfortable and secure compromise, an excellent choice for touring.

Whatever type of spray skirt you choose, make sure it fits. Don't be convinced that the one or two models at your local shop will necessarily fit your

spray skirt

boat. Buy one on the condition that it can be returned if it doesn't work out. Then take it home and try these tests to see if it fits you and the boat.

Without you in it, put the skirt on the boat and then try to pick up the kayak by the skirt's tunnel. A skirt that is too loose will slip right off, one that is too tight will hold on forever. A skirt with a good fit will hold the boat for a few seconds and then slowly lose its grip. Another test is to put the spray skirt on, get in the boat, and seal the skirt around the coaming. Now draw your knees up and try to stand. The skirt should resist but eventually come free. A good spray skirt also must not hinder your movements. Leaning all the way forward, back, and to the sides should not cause it to come off. To see how the spray skirt will stand up to a breaking wave, put it on the boat while wet. If the fit is correct, it will not pop off when given a good solid thump at its center. Be particularly wary when fitting a skirt to a polyethylene plastic kayak: the coamings on these are very slippery and need spray skirts that have special neoprene or rubber strips to help maintain a grip.

The proper way to use a spray skirt is to step into it, pull it up as high as you can, and then roll up the rear hem of the skirt before boarding the boat. Once seated, roll down the hem in the back and stretch it over the rear coaming. Next, stretch the skirt over the front coaming and then seal the remaining sides. Make sure that the elastic in the hem is pushed all the way under the coaming lip and that the grab loop at the front has not been tucked under the skirt. This is your rip cord for a fast escape, and it should be right there when you need it. To release the spray skirt, first pull the grab loop forward and then up. Pulling straight up or straight back puts a strain on the stitching and increases wear on the front edge of the skirt. To free the rest of the skirt, run your fingers along the inside of the coaming to release the elastic all the way around. If in an emergency you find that you cannot locate the grab loop, lean to one side, grab the folds that will gather at that side, and pull up.

PFD

On most vessels a person puts on a PFD—personal flotation device—only when the boat is about to sink. Although it is unlikely your kayak will sink, it could capsize; then you will need all the buoyancy you can get. Capsizes happen suddenly and trying to get into a PFD in the water while holding onto the kayak and paddle is almost impossible. PFDs work for you while you're still in the kayak, too. If you try to prevent a capsize, or do go over and attempt an Eskimo roll, a PFD might give you that extra flotation to make it back up. A close-fitting PFD also acts as an insulating layer in the water and in the air. All very good reasons to wear yours every time out.

The U.S. Coast Guard certifies several categories of PFDs. Most sea kayakers choose a type 3, which was created for sport use and, if designed properly, can be ideal for kayaking. Because they are meant to support an active paddler and not an unconscious castaway, the U.S. Coast Guard prefers manufacturers to call them "flotation aids" and not "life jackets." Either way, they guarantee a minimum of 15½ pounds of flotation, and some have more, which is plenty for our purposes. The deciding factor in choosing a PFD is fit.

When shopping, remember that a PFD is always the outermost garment and will be worn over a variety of clothing. Make sure that there is enough adjustability to go over a sweater and paddling jacket, a wet suit, or only a T-shirt. It should be a snug fit but not to the extent that it restricts any head, body, or arm motions. You may find that the ones made of narrow, vertical foam panels are less rigid than the ones that are solid slabs. Those that provide flotation all the way around the body, including the sides, are better insulators. They are also the ones most likely to restrict arm motions. Try a few windmills and thrash about with your arms; if you make frequent rubbing contact with the PFD in the store, it will probably mean chafing on the water.

PFD length will be limited by your spray skirt. One that is too long will be forced up around your ears. The "shorty" type that comes down to your last rib is the right length for kayak use but may be bulky. Another type has lower panels that roll up and flare out on top of the skirt. These are less bulky but can form a semirigid structure that prevents easy movement, especially toward the back.

Check for adequate fasteners such as belts and ties to keep the PFD from riding up around you while in the water. You can test this on land by putting your arms over your head and having someone push up on the bottom. Ties should be of a quick-release type that can be worked with cold, wet fingers.

If you want your PFD to last for several years, do not sit on it or put heavy weights, such as the kayak, on it. Each time the foam is compressed, buoyancy is reduced. Heat and sunlight also degrade flotation. A natural attrition of 3 percent per year means that every few years you should consider getting a new PFD. If you capsize and find yourself floating with your nose underwater, it's probably time to buy another.

Thinking about improving your PFD? Be careful. Almost anything you do to it will void its coast guard approval. What you can do is tie a whistle to the zipper pull, cut belts to length, or add reflective adhesive tape. What you cannot do is stitch anything to the PFD. If your PFD has a pocket without a drain hole, make one. This will not affect the PFD's performance except for the better, although it will probably void the approval. But don't worry, I'll never tell them you did it.

Audible Signal

The coast guard also recommends that you carry "any device capable of making an efficient sound signal audible for ½ nautical mile." The main purpose of this is to warn anyone with whom you happen to be sharing the water that you are there. Being so low in the water, sea kayaks have a way of becoming invisible to operators of sail- and motor-

PFD

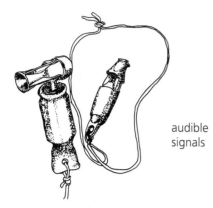

audible
signals

boats. A secondary use is for communication between kayaks traveling together.

You could conceivably get away with a whistle, and there are some available that technically meet coast guard requirements, but their range is limited. If purchasing a police-type whistle, make sure that the "pea" will not disintegrate in water.

For a few dollars more you can get a small gas-charged horn from a bicycle or marine supply store. This type of horn has a range of up to 1 mile, weighs only a few ounces, fits in the palm of your hand, and gives about 100 blasts per replaceable cartridge (keep a spare on board). It is best stowed in an accessible garment pocket or on deck so it is immediately available when needed.

Putting things under the bungee cords on deck is handy, but far from secure. A solution for your mini horn is to slide the canister into a section of bicycle tire inner tube, leaving a little tube left over. Then punch a hole in the excess inner tube and thread a short piece of line through the hole. Tie the line to something secure and trap the horn under the bungees. The line will keep it from being washed overboard and the rubber tube will keep the canister from scratching the deck

Bailers

Kayaks are supposed to be watertight boats; this is what ensures their ultimate safety. But nothing with openings can be made absolutely waterproof, so from time to time you'll be sharing your kayak with varying amounts of water.

Typically the most you will have to deal with is a small drip from a leaky fitting, hatch, or spray skirt. For this there is nothing better than a sponge. Both aesthetically and pragmatically, the best sponge you

can get is a large natural one. They are more absorbent, tougher, and softer to the touch than synthetic sponges. Next best is your basic synthetic bilge sponge from a marine supply store. Make it the biggest and roundest you can find. All sponges have a way of getting lost, especially if the boat happens to fill with water. Make sure to secure the sponge with a short length of line passed through it to the boat.

When your kayak does fill with water, you'll want to empty it as quickly as possible, and very often you will be doing this while swimming alongside. The easiest and cheapest way to bail is with a plastic container such as a drink pitcher. Fishermen have been using old bleach bottles for decades; take a cue from them. Get one that is round, as rigid as possible, has a good-size handle, and a cap that screws on and will not rust, then cut the bottom off. Like the sponge, make sure your bailer is secured to the boat.

You can also use the plastic bailer while in the boat, but this entails pulling back the spray skirt, which will invite even more water in on a rough day. To empty the kayak with the skirt on you have three options: an electric pump, a deck-mounted hand pump, or a handheld pump.

For those who love gadgets and don't mind spending money, there are small, self-contained electric bilge pumps specifically made for kayaks. They are easy to use and the larger ones move a good stream of water; but they bring the problems

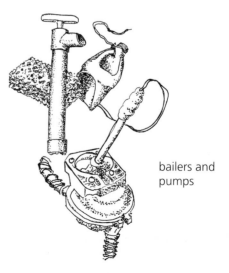

bailers and
pumps

of additional weight, installation, and maintenance.

Many British kayaks come with a diaphragm pump mounted on the aft deck, and there is no reason why you can't add one to your boat. The advantages of these pumps are that they are always there when you need them, they can be operated with only one hand, and it is almost impossible to clog them. The disadvantage is that many models displace small amounts of water for the effort expended; try before you buy.

The cheapest and most common method of pumping is with a handheld model. To use it, you simply stick it down the front of the spray skirt's tunnel and pump away. Typically these are 18-inch plastic bilge pumps that are tough, lightweight, and, depending on the model, can move from 6 to 10 gallons per minute. You'll find a variety of pump lengths, but remember that although a longer pump moves more water, using it may be awkward. The problem with handheld pumps is that they require two hands, one to hold the pump and the other to do the work; however, they work fine if you can raft up with another kayak for stability. Another problem is that these pumps sink when full of water. To avoid this, attach a ring of foam (such as that used to insulate pipes) and secure it to the pump with glue or tape.

Once you have ensured that it won't sink, you have to keep it from floating away. Many paddlers stick their pumps between the seat support and the side of the boat; this is a good safe place. Do not stow it under a bungee cord on deck because it might come free in a capsize. Wherever you stow it, make sure it is accessible yet secure.

Bow Line

There are times when you will need to tie up your kayak while on land or be towed by another vessel while at sea. For both instances do not expect someone else to supply the line. Bring your own and keep it rigged and ready.

A bow line can be permanently installed by tying one end of ¼-inch (minimum) nylon or Dacron line to a secure fitting on the bow of your kayak. This can be the fitting through which the grab loop is run or it can be the grab loop itself. Attach the line using a figure-eight loop knot, leaving a loop that is large enough for more line to be passed through it. Lead the free end of the line back to a fitting (such as an eye

figure-eight
loop knot

strap used to hold down a bungee) to one side of the cockpit. Pass the line through this fitting, back up to the loop at the bow, and then back to a fitting on the other side of the cockpit. Pass the line through this last fitting and make it fast on itself with a trucker's hitch (see page 35).

This rig will give you two working lengths. If you only let go of the line secured to the second fitting, it will be one-third its length. If you let go of the line and then pull it back through the bow loop and the first fitting by the cockpit, you have use of the full length.

Paddle Float

A hundred and fifty years ago it was recorded that the Aleutian kayakers did not know of, or use, what we now call an *Eskimo roll* to right a capsized kayak. Instead they would use the inflated stomach of a sea lion to help them right and reenter their boat. Thankfully you no longer need to find a suitable animal bladder to do this. Paddle floats in lovely man-made materials are now available.

When modern sea kayakers try to reenter their capsized boats they can inflate a bag-like device, slip it over a paddle blade, and then either jam the other blade under lines that have been specifically rigged behind the cockpit or hold the blade in place. When set up like this, the float and paddle act like an outrigger, greatly enhancing the kayak's stability. It is then easier for you to climb up on and back into the kayak. Once you're in the boat and it is bailed out, the float can be removed by releasing the air.

Paddle floats are made by different companies but all work on the same principle. There are homemade versions in which collapsible plastic jugs are used; these are complicated and probably not worth the risk for the few dollars saved. One alternative is a closed-cell foam block. This does not need inflating, can be used as an aid for practicing braces and rolling, but takes up a lot of room on deck.

Flotation

The primary idea behind every boat, even a kayak, is to float you and whatever else you put in it. If your kayak (which is probably made of a nonbuoyant material) somehow becomes filled with water, it will either sink or flounder hopelessly out of balance. This is a situation that must be prevented at all costs.

The solution is to exclude water from every unused space. The only place that should be open to water is where you sit, and even this must be kept to a minimum. The goal is to stay afloat while in the kayak, even when it is completely flooded. You also want to remain on an even keel and keep the cockpit coaming high enough to prevent more water from coming in. This will require approximately 70 pounds of positive flotation evenly distributed fore and aft.

The most common method of doing this in sea kayaks is with watertight bulkheads. These may come as standard equipment or as an option, and are installed fore and aft of the cockpit. They may be made of fiberglass, plastic, or foam panels, and are fiberglassed in place or held in with caulking. Almost all caulked bulkheads eventually leak. Check yours at the start of each season and reseal with a polyurethane sealant, if necessary.

Bulkheads create convenient stowage compartments accessible through a variety of hatches. Like bulkheads, hatches also eventually leak. Sometimes simply cleaning the seal or adding neoprene gaskets will help; sometimes there is just nothing you can do. Luckily the amount they leak is usually very little, but as a backup you might want to keep your gear in watertight bags, called *dry bags*, which in themselves act as reserve buoyancy.

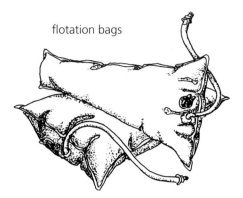
flotation bags

Many boats have no bulkheads or other form of built-in flotation and will therefore require inflatable flotation bags. These come in a variety of materials, sizes, and shapes. Some can double as gear stowage bags. Whatever type you use, make sure that they fill up as much space as possible both fore and aft of the cockpit. It will be easier to do this if they are shaped to fit and have extra-long inflating tubes so that they can be inflated in place. Before installing bags, check that the inside skin of the kayak has no rough spots and that the bags can be held securely in place. Inflatable bags belong in collapsible kayaks, too. Even though these boats may have air chambers, they may not have enough reserve buoyancy to float themselves with you in them.

An interesting backup to bulkheads and inflatable bags is the Sea Sock. This is a large bag that encloses the lower body and is sealed around the coaming. It tends to feel warm, slippery, and clinging, and takes some getting used to. Although a Sea Sock does substantially limit the amount of water that can enter the kayak, it should not be thought of as a primary line of defense.

Eyeglass Strap

As a kayaker you will spend most of your time right side up, but there will be instances when practicing or by accident that you will find yourself in the water. If this happens, make sure you come back up with your glasses by using one of the many popular straps.

Nose Clips

While practicing, you'll be spending some time underwater, often at unusual angles. Plain, old-fashioned nose clips from a sporting goods store are just the thing to keep your head clear and your sinuses free of seaweed.

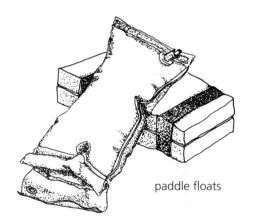
paddle floats

A PLACE TO LEARN

Where you learn has a great impact on your early success and future abilities. The place you choose should be a sanctuary: a place to which you can conveniently return again and again for practice and for working things out. It's your home base. Get your maneuvers right there and you'll be able to take them with you wherever you go.

It is best to learn in an environment similar to the one in which you will be doing most of your paddling. Quiet, easily accessible beaches are ideal. Make sure that hard, sharp objects are scarce and that the water is clean and deepens gradually. Shallow areas (less than 2 feet deep) give a feeling of security when first starting out and are good for experiments in leaning and bracing. A little farther out (at least 4 feet deep) will be perfect for practicing rolling, paddling, and anything else. Try to find a beach protected from the wind, which brings waves and chills. It's nice to have your car parked nearby; it's a place to relax, think, and warm up. If possible, practice in water warmer than 65°F. When you can't, or when you will be wet for prolonged periods, wear clothing that will prevent the loss of body heat such as a thin wet suit, or at least a Lycra top.

Docks, too, are handy for learning. Find one that is low in the water, preferably a floating dock with rubrails around it. A dock in a swimming area or marina might be available after hours, but be mindful of boat traffic and its resulting wakes.

KRCKA EXPEDITIONS

If you have access to one, a swimming pool can also be a good place to learn. But consider a few things before jumping in. For one, kayaks need to be cleaned before being used in a pool. The little bits of sand, muck, and other debris from the outside world must be removed to preserve the pool's plumbing and health rating. Kayaks and paddles can scratch or otherwise mar the pool and themselves. To prevent this you can use a polyethylene plastic boat, which is less apt to damage itself and its surroundings. As an extra precaution, bumpers, in the form of foam padding, can be duct-taped to the bow and stern. You probably won't be able to practice in your own boat because sea kayaks are usually too long and difficult to turn in a pool. So you'll more than likely need to find a smaller whitewater slalom boat.

There's another factor to consider. Emerging from the cloistered haven of a pool to the real world requires a certain amount of relearning, or at least adapting to a new environment. Tides, currents, winds, and weather must all be considered in sea kayaking. If they are present from the beginning, although not so much as to be overwhelming, you'll develop a better sense of what sea kayaking is all about.

This is not to condemn pool sessions. They have a definite place for those whose weather is not always hospitable. In the winter they are godsends for keeping the rust off your hard-won skills. But as soon as the weather breaks, it is probably best to go elsewhere. Work done in a pool must supplement, not replace, practice under natural conditions.

Your practice time for specific maneuvers will vary. If you encounter difficulty with what you are doing, stop and return to something familiar. Once comfortable with a maneuver, leave the safety of your practice sanctuary and set out onto open waters to experience what you have learned. If it doesn't feel right, don't push yourself and don't worry, you can always return to your practice sanctuary.

MEET YOUR KAYAK

LIFTING

Considering how graceful sea kayaks are on the water, it is often surprising how clumsy they can be on land. But, as with almost everything related to this sport, lifting and carrying a kayak is more a matter of technique than strength and, once learned, should present no problems.

The easiest method of carrying a kayak involves two people, one at each end, using the grab loops, toggles, or ends of the boat. Make sure that all heavy gear has been removed from the boat, especially from the center section.

Carrying a kayak on your own is more difficult and may even seem hopeless if the boat is heavy. But after a few tries you'll find it can be easily done.

With the boat empty, find the balance point along its length. It should be just a little forward of the seat. Mark this spot on both sides of the cockpit coaming.

To lift the boat, squat down, keeping your feet shoulder-width apart and pointing slightly outward. Make sure your back stays straight. Grab the coaming closest to you with each hand equidistant from the balance point. Pull the boat up against your shins so its side is on the ground (photo 1). From this position straighten up in one smooth motion. Use your legs to lift, letting the momentum bring your back to the vertical while pulling up slightly with your arms. This will hoist the kayak to waist height, where it can be carried for short distances (2).

To raise the boat from here onto your shoulder, get an underhand grip on the lower coaming with one hand. Using the hand on the upper coaming as a pivot point, bring the lower hand toward you and upward while simultaneously lifting the boat with the knee and thigh of one leg (3). If this is done in a rapid and forceful manner, you should be able to fling the boat high enough to slip your shoulder under the coaming.

To stabilize the boat while carrying it, slide your shoulder slightly behind the balance point. Then bring the hand from your carrying side to the coaming, or somewhere inside the boat, to a position just ahead of the balance point (4). Use your other hand to guide the boat and keep it from being blown about. Lower the kayak by reversing the procedure, using your raised thigh to help ease it toward the ground.

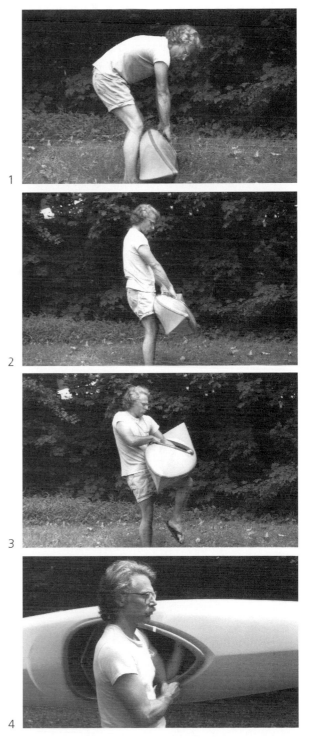

1

2

3

4

MAKING IT FIT

Manufacturers build their kayaks to accommodate as wide a variety of body types as possible. So it is a rare new boat that provides a perfect fit. As with the tailoring of a suit, it is easier to reduce something that is too large than to increase the size of something that is too small. If you have to jam your hips into the seat or twist your feet and knees outward at excruciatingly oblique angles, get a boat with more room. Conversely, if you feel like a bug in a tub, look for a more compact boat. The initial fit should be at least reasonably close.

Don't be afraid to make adjustments and changes to your boat. If you are careful, you will not irrevocably damage or ruin it. All you'll need is some closed-cell foam (which is commonly available from kayaking suppliers), a knife, a hacksaw, some sandpaper, and an adhesive. For fiberglass boats, plain contact cement is fine. Polyethylene plastic boats may need special adhesives, so ask the dealer or builder first.

The purpose of a good fit is to provide comfort and improve control and efficiency by transmitting the forces generated by the body-paddle combination directly to the boat. You want to be able to make solid contact with your feet, knees, hips, rear, and back. The fit should be loose enough for comfort, yet close enough so that by flexing your feet and thighs you become one with the kayak.

The balls of your feet are the direct transmitters of forward forces from the body-paddle to the kayak. Adjust the foot pedals or bar so that your knees are touching the underside of the deck and your lower back, from the waist down, is gently pressed into the back of the seat or backrest. Your heels should be close together, your toes turned outward, and your feet at not quite 90 degrees to your ankles. Sit this way for fifteen minutes. If your feet or legs go to sleep, give yourself more room.

Balancing and leaning forces are directed through the knees. The farther apart you can place your knees without being uncomfortable, the better your side-to-side balance will be. They should just touch the deck near the sides of the boat. If their angle feels comfortable and not cramped or awkward, place some thin padding on the underside of the deck as a cushion. If they do not make contact with the deck, add thicker pieces of foam as spacers. Tape the foam into place first and paddle that way for a while before gluing it. In addition to your knees, some boats let you brace the upper part of your thighs against the coaming. These areas may also need some padding.

Your hips help you control and balance the boat, functions they can best fulfill if you are not sliding around on the seat. To keep yourself in place, put foam blocks between your hips and the sides of the boat. Do not pack yourself in so tightly that you have trouble getting in or out of the boat, or that an extra layer of clothing will affect the fit. Leave ½ to ¾ inch on either side.

Pressing your feet and legs forward will be for naught if there is nothing to stop you from sliding backward. Both the seat and the back support help you lock yourself in and transmit the body-paddle forces that stop, slow, or reverse the boat. A back support usually takes the form of a seatback or cushioned strap. It should not be thought of as a backrest on which to relax. If your boat's seatback extends too far above your lower back, it will restrict upper body motion and should be changed.

Finally there is the seat, which should be as low as possible to gain overall stability, but not so low as to be detrimental to your paddling. It should provide friction to keep you from sliding around and should be sloped at the same angle as your thighs to give them support. It would be nice if it were soft, too.

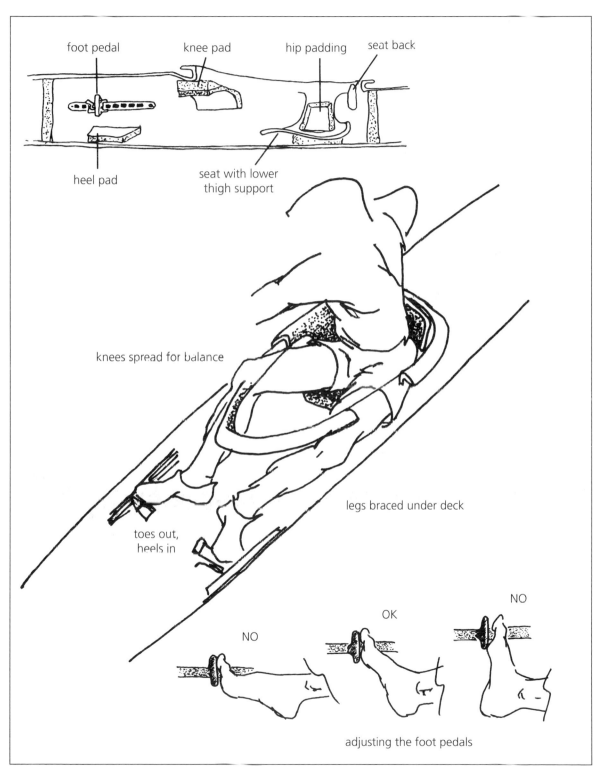

foot pedal   knee pad   hip padding   seat back

heel pad

seat with lower
thigh support

knees spread for balance

legs braced under deck

toes out,
heels in

NO   OK   NO

adjusting the foot pedals

TRANSPORTING BY CAR

Hoisting a 60-pound kayak onto your cartop need not resemble an Olympic weight-lifting event. Instead of lifting it all at once, do it in stages, starting from the ground or a shoulder carry.

Depending on your car's shape and the height of its roof, you can put the kayak on the car from behind or from the side. When loading from the rear, which works best on tall vehicles, place the kayak on the ground so that 4 feet of its bow is off to one side and the stern is directly behind the car. Put a towel or blanket under the stern if you want to prevent scratches. Lift the bow and place it on the rear rack. Walk to the stern and lift and push the boat into place. If the boat does not slide easily, you will have to advance it by lifting and moving in short stages. Be patient and you'll do it. To make this type of loading easier, some rack manufacturers make boat saddles with rollers that lock tight after you slide the kayak on from the rear.

For the side lift, place the boat about 4 feet from the car so that the bow extends beyond the front rack by approximately 6 feet. Lift the bow onto the front rack. If only a short length makes it on, lift the kayak by its middle section to move it farther forward. When set, lift the stern into place.

Once your kayak is up, you have to keep it there. To do this, the boat has to be supported from underneath and secured in place at its middle and ends.

Ideally, support should come from a rack with either horizontal cradles that distribute the weight and are low enough to make loading easy, or vertical J cradles or stacker bars that require you to lift the boat higher but let it rest on its side, which is its strongest point. An alternative for short trips is thick, resilient padding over crossbars. Regardless of the type, racks should be as close to 5 feet apart as possible. This spreads support and keeps the widest section of the kayak between the tie-down points to prevent slipping.

Straps that cross over the boat are the best tie-downs. These minimize chafe and distribute their hold over a wider area than rope. When used with self-locking, cam-type buckles, an amazingly tight and tenacious grip can be achieved. But don't overdo it. You could crack a fiberglass boat, deform a polyethylene plastic one, or make a mess out of coamings and hatches by overtightening.

Nylon or Dacron rope should be used for tying the ends of the kayak to prevent lifting and lateral movement; do not use bungee cords (too stretchy) or polypropylene rope (too slippery). Lines should form an inverted V from the kayak's ends to each side of the front and back of the car. The best knots for this job are the bowline, which makes a fixed loop that will not jam, and a trucker's hitch, which makes an adjustable loop to provide tension. Lines should be attached to the kayak and then to any point on the car that will not chafe through the rope. On a car without bumpers, straps often can be closed under the hood or trunk lid. Enough strap is left sticking out so that a loop can be tied in it to provide something to which to fasten the ropes.

Kayaks on cartops should be kept empty of heavy equipment, facing forward, and closed to the elements. Gear can fly out at high speeds, or its weight, as well as the weight of collected rain, can strain the boat as it bounces down the road. Even cockpit covers can blow off and should be secured with a safety line just in case.

Top right: Rear Loading. Cushion the stern, lift the bow, and push the kayak into place.

Center right: Side Loading. Cushion the stern, place bow on the rack, and lift the stern onto the rack.

Bottom right: Two knots you'll need to secure your kayak.

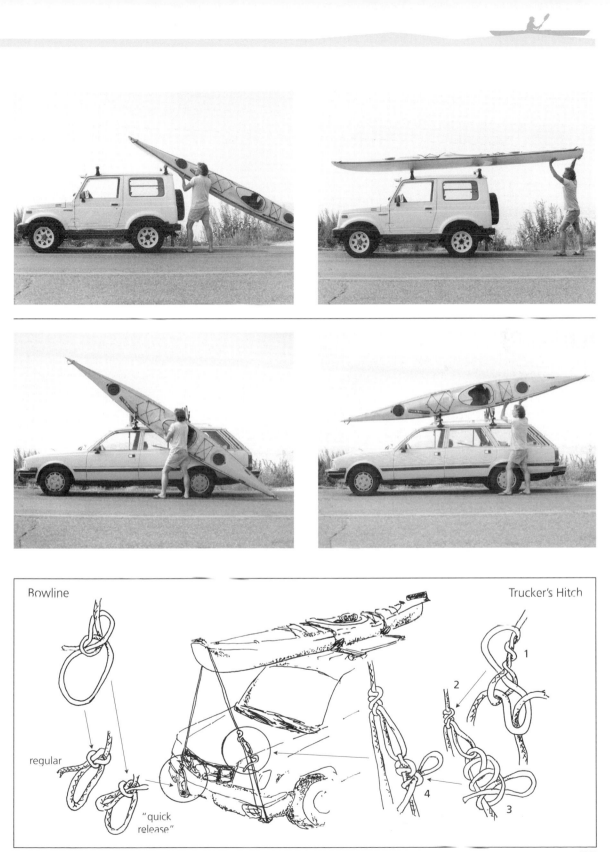

Bowline

Trucker's Hitch

regular

"quick release"

1

2

3

4

TRANSPORTING BY HAND

Occasionally you may need to transport your kayak a considerable distance by hand. For example, you may have to park your car three or four blocks from a dock, or you may be traveling by ferry between islands during a multiday trip.

It's feasible for a strong person to hand-carry a boat for a few blocks, but if the wind is blowing (and it usually is by the sea), having an 18-foot-long wind vane draped over your shoulder is not fun. Two people can carry a boat for long distances—one at the bow, one at the stern—but the strain on the backs, hands, and arms of both parties should be taken into account. A number of companies make small kayak carts that strap to the stern or under a bulkhead, and you simply pull the boat with the carrying toggle on the bow.

JONATHAN HANSEN

Proper care of your boat and gear will make them last a long time; many wood and fiberglass kayaks are still in service after decades of use and tender loving care.

First, rinse everything well inside and out with fresh water after any use. Spray skirts, dry bags, and PFDs can be dunked in a tub of fresh water. This is the time to give everything the once over for damage that should be repaired. Check rudder lines, deck rigging, bulkheads, straps, and seams on your PFD and spray skirt, paddle blades, and so on. (See the section on resources for recommended books on gear care and repair.)

Dry everything thoroughly out of direct sunlight before storing it. All types of boats should be stored in a clean, dry area out of sunlight—which hastens the deterioration of fiberglass and plastic. Do not wrap any boat in a plastic tarp; it will rapidly become a petri dish for all sorts of interesting members of the kingdom Fungi. If you need to use a tarp for sun and rain protection, rig it a foot or more away from the hull.

Use the same principles of supporting your boat in storage as you do in transportation: cradle it under the bulkheads or on its side. Take particular care to support a plastic boat well or its hull will take a new shape that cannot be changed. Some people hang boats from slings in their carports or garages; others build special boat houses for them. Keep hatches open to prevent the growth of damaging mildew and mold. If possible, store folding kayaks out of the bags, loosely rolled or folded (every few months change the fold to a different part of the hull so permanent creases do not form); under a bed is a good spot for storing a folding boat.

Store your soft goods (such as your PFD and spray skirt) in a closet if possible to protect them from dust, mold, and heat. Roll them loosely and lay them on a shelf or hang them; spray skirts can be damaged if folded and flattened. Store inflatable paddle floats and flotation bags partially inflated. Paddle blades should be protected from dings, so a good place for them is a closet or under a bed. Roll them in an old blanket, or invest in a padded paddle bag.

A good tenet to live by: Take care of your gear and it will take care of you.

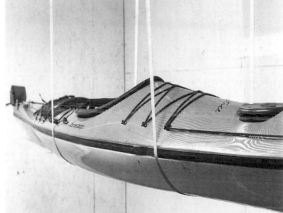

DOUG HAYWARD

GETTING IN AND OUT (DRY)

BEACH: KAYAK IN WATER

Your center of gravity is at its highest in relation to the kayak when getting in or out. So there's no wonder that the kayak, and you, are most unstable during these procedures. This is where most beginners take their first dunking.

To avoid this, use the paddle as a stabilizing bar, sort of like an 8-foot-long kickstand. It's easy to do, but if you're feeling a little anxious or clumsy, you might first try the procedure on a grassy lawn to prove to yourself that it really works.

This type of entry and exit requires the kayak to be close-in and parallel to shore. If the wind is blowing onto the beach with any strength, or if there is excessive wave action, you will have to forgo this procedure and use the kayak-on-land technique.

Before starting, put on all your protective clothing, then the spray skirt if you're using one, and finally your PFD. Roll up the back hem of the spray skirt so you won't sit on it. With the kayak afloat in 6 inches of calm water to minimize damage to its bottom, bring it alongside the beach. Stand in the water between the boat and the shore, with your face toward the bow. Place your paddle behind your back and lay its shaft across the boat's aft deck, just behind the coaming and perpendicular to the boat's

centerline. The boatside blade should be just past the side of the kayak, the shoreside blade resting flat on the beach. To prevent damage, the power face of a curved blade resting on the shore should be upward.

Using the hand closest to the boat, hold the paddle shaft against the aft coaming with your fingers inside the coaming and your thumb around the shaft. Place the hand closest to the shore on the shaft just outboard of the boat's side, using the same sort of backhanded grip. As much as possible, avoid placing too much strain on the paddle. It should only have to take the minimum amount of weight necessary for you to keep your balance.

With the paddle in position, sit down on the aft deck. Bring one leg in at a time while leaning toward shore to prevent tipping (illustration 1). Depending on the size of your cockpit, you now either lower your rear down to the seat with your knees bent, or work your legs under the deck until they are far enough in that you can lower your rear onto the seat.

Once in (illustration 2), bring the paddle around front, secure it so it won't float off, and then snap on your spray skirt. To exit the kayak, repeat the procedure in reverse.

BEACH: KAYAK ON LAND

There will be times when the water is too rough or the bottom drops away too abruptly for you to be able to get into the boat while it is in the water. When this happens, you will have to get in on land and "walk" the kayak, with you in it, to the water.

Because you'll want to keep your walk short, it is best to put the boat down as close to the water's edge as possible. This might be an area in the surf's wash or a spot where the bow is at least in the water. Naturally you'll be facing bow out, perpendicular to the beach; and naturally you'll pick as soft a spot as possible for the sake of your boat's bottom.

If you're still feeling wary about your kayak, or have a boat that is tippy even on land (as are some V-bottomed boats), you can steady the boat by using your paddle as a brace, being careful not to damage the blades. If it is not necessary to brace the boat, you can step right in and sit down, support your weight with your hands on the aft coaming and bring your legs in one at a time, or sit on the aft deck and do the same thing. Be careful with this last method; some polyethylene plastic boats may be dented (but should pop right back) if too much weight is put on the deck. Whichever way you use to get in, you might want to knock off as much sand or mud as possible before bringing your feet into the boat. It's always better if you can avoid sitting in grit.

Once in, and with the spray skirt in place, you can begin your march to the sea. But before doing anything, make sure that you secure your paddle. Then, using your fists against the ground, reach down with both hands and push (photo 1). At the same time try to bring your knees up and swing yourself forward. In

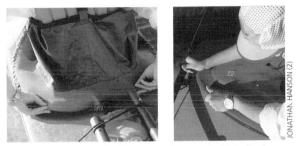

When you are ready to secure the spray skirt, fit the back first, then run the bead along to the front, making sure the grab loop is outside.

this turtle-like fashion you will eventually reach the water with a minimum amount of scarring to your boat.

Some find using their fists uncomfortable. If that's the case, you can curl your knuckles in like an orangutan and walk on them. Try to avoid the more human-like way of using your outspread hands to do the pushing. Although it seems the more logical approach, it may actually be pulling an unnecessary strain on your wrists.

If your arms are not long enough for this sort of travel, you can use your fist or knuckles on one side and the paddle on the other (photo 2). Your fist will take most of the weight while the paddle acts like a cane for the opposite side.

You'll want to get yourself afloat as fast and completely as possible. If you don't, there is a chance of being hung up with your bow in the water and stern on land, which is a very unstable position. If caught like this, push or paddle your way into deeper water and be ready to brace with your paddle.

LOW DOCK

As populations grow and beach access decreases, more of us will be doing our kayaking from public launching ramps. If your ramp area isn't crowded or its surface isn't too rough, you could get in and out of the boat as if from a beach. But if the place is popular, or you don't want to grind your paddle blade to splinters on the concrete, you'll need to know how to use a dock. Because launching ramps are meant for small boats, docks there are usually low to the water.

To a kayak, a low dock is anything that is close to, or below, the level of the coaming. With a dock, or anything else, of this height, you can use the paddle as a supporting brace.

Start by sitting as close to the edge of the dock as possible and facing the bow of the boat. Put the paddle behind you, laying the shaft across the boat's aft deck just to the rear of the coaming. The outboard blade should be just past the side of the boat and the other blade should be resting flat on the dock, with the power face up for curved blades. Hold the paddle shaft against the coaming and place your other hand on the dock. Try to put as little weight on the shaft as possible. With most of your weight supported by your legs and the hand on the dock, bring one leg in at a time, and then lower yourself onto the seat (photo 1, right).

There are also techniques that do not use a paddle for support. One requires you to start in the seated position as above. Keep the paddle nearby so it can be reached once you're in. Put both feet on the centerline. Use your arms to lift yourself off the dock, swing your rear over the boat, and lower your-

JONATHAN HANSON

At small but busy launch ramps, such as this one in Telegraph Cove, British Columbia, load and launch your boat to one side if possible, so you don't clog it up for other boaters.

paddle as brace

from seated position

from squatting position

self onto the seat. Your upper body weight must be kept over the dock and supported by your arms during the procedure (photo 2).

Another way is to squat down near the edge of the dock facing the bow of the boat. While supporting yourself with your legs and the hand on the dock, take hold of the front coaming. Keeping your weight over the dock, swing the leg closest to the boat into the cockpit, putting your foot just to the far side of the centerline. Now, with most of your weight over the hand on the dock, swing the other leg into the boat and settle down onto the seat (photo 3).

All three procedures are equally valid. It's your choice. The size or shape of some cockpits may make it impossible for you to lower yourself directly onto the seat. When this occurs, place your feet in the cockpit as before, but lower your rear to the aft deck. Once seated there, lift up a little, straighten your legs, and wriggle down onto the seat.

No matter how you get in, remember to roll up the back of your spray skirt before entering the boat. Trying to reach behind to get it out from under you could result in a dunking. Do this slowly and carefully.

Exiting the kayak is simply a matter of reversing these procedures. However, you may find that the technique that worked best to get you into the boat is not necessarily the one you can use to get out. Experiment.

HIGH DOCK

To a kayak, a high dock is anything above the level of the coaming. This means that it is too far above the boat for you to either lean over and steady it or to use your paddle as a supporting brace. Anything over 3 to 4 feet from the water is too high. The determining factor is how far up you can comfortably reach while seated in the boat.

To gauge the probability for success of entering your boat from a high dock, sit on the very edge and hang your legs over the side. If you must stretch to make your toes reach the cockpit floor, you're flirting with trouble and should try to find some place lower. For a dock that is within your range though, getting in and out may take a little effort but should not be all that difficult.

First, put your paddle down so you can reach it when in the boat. Then sit on the edge of the dock with your feet holding the kayak in place (photo 1, below). Twist your body so you are facing the bow, place both hands on the dock ahead and slightly to one side, push up to lift your rear, and then roll over on your front. Now, with your body leaning over the dock, your rear suspended over the boat, and your feet on the centerline of the cockpit, slowly lower yourself onto the seat bending your knees as you descend (photo 2).

During this procedure keep as much weight on your hands as possible. Trying to support too much weight with your feet will cause the boat to move, leaving you hanging in space.

It may be impossible to lower yourself directly onto the seat in the cockpits of some boats. When this occurs, place your feet in the cockpit as before, but lower your rear to the aft deck. Once seated there, lift up a little, straighten your legs, and wriggle down onto the seat.

To get out of the boat, you use the same procedure in reverse. The only problem you might encounter is that your arms may not be strong enough to pull yourself up. If this is the case, bring your knees up so your feet are near your rear end or get up on to the aft deck with your feet in the cockpit. From this position your legs can help a little. But don't try to stand. This will cause the boat to go one way and you another. Let your arms do most of the work. If you can manage to get your upper torso over the edge of the dock, it will be possible to drag the rest of you behind it. Not very elegant, but it works.

The higher the dock, the more you will have to rely on your sense of balance and the strength of your arms. Consider wind and waves, too. It might be worth going a little out of your way to find a slightly lower dock.

GETTING OUT AND IN (WET)

WET EXIT

To those who have never experienced it, the prospect of a capsize may conjure up fears of being trapped upside down underwater. Once it happens, however, the reality is almost a let-down. There's nothing to it.

The fact is that in a properly fitted kayak, the pressure of your feet, thighs, and hips against the boat holds you in. Relax this pressure and, in most boats, when you're upside down you'll almost fall out. The worst that can happen is that you'll get water up your nose, which can easily be prevented with a nose clip.

Practice wet exits in water that is at least 4 feet deep, wearing your PFD, and with a friend standing nearby, if only for moral support. For these first attempts do not bother with a spray skirt or your paddle.

Once upside down try to relax, using pressure from your legs to hold you in. Force yourself to bang on the bottom of the boat three times or do anything else that will postpone a hasty escape. The complete exit takes only two seconds, whereas the average person can hold his or her breath for thirty. So time is on your side.

To exit, place both hands on the kayak next to your hips, ease the grip of your legs and straighten them to help you slip out, use your arms to push, and curl forward as in a somersault. Once up, make sure that you keep a firm hold on the kayak; this should become second nature so, if you capsize and wet exit in rough water, you minimize the chance of being permanently separated from your boat.

Now try the same thing with a spray skirt in place. When putting it on, make sure that the release strap is readily accessible. Practice releasing the skirt while upright. Then go out and capsize, hang there to collect your thoughts, pull and lift the release strap, check the skirt to see that it has released, then roll out as before. There may come a time when the release strap is missing or mistakenly tucked under. To get free, lean to one side, grab the bunched up material on that side, and lift it away from the coaming.

Next try an exit with your paddle. Capsize while holding it in both hands. Once upside down, hold on with one hand and use the other to deal with the skirt and push out from the boat. Come to the surface with the paddle, gripping the boat with your other hand. Never let either go adrift.

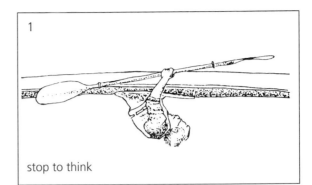

1 stop to think

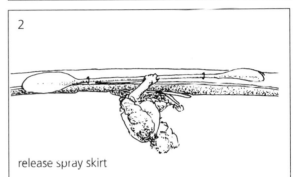

2 release spray skirt

3 push out

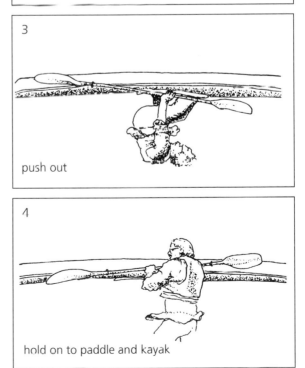

4 hold on to paddle and kayak

SWIMMING

Although swimming with your kayak is not a common activity, it is something that must be learned. If for some reason you find yourself out of the boat, the most desirable option is usually to get back in. But sometimes this is not possible or, if you are very close to shore, not even desirable.

Before learning to swim with a kayak there are some basic rules of safety to keep in mind.

First, and most important, is that you should be able to swim at least 200 feet on your own. Every paddler must be a reasonably good swimmer. You need not have great style or be able to swim long distances, just be good enough to feel confident in and under the water. No matter how accomplished a swimmer you might be, it is almost always safest to stick with the boat in case of an emergency. A kayak, even one that is partially swamped, will provide extra flotation and be easier to spot than a lone swimmer.

There is also the nature of kayaks to consider. Partially flooded kayaks can often drift much faster than you would expect, and a gentle breeze can push an empty one well ahead of even the best swimmer. So always keep hold of your boat and, when you must let go, stay on its downwind side. There is an exception to this rule and that is when you are in surf or breaking seas. In these situations, try to maintain your hold while staying upwind or up-wave of the boat so it won't hit you.

No matter what the sea's condition, you'll be best off if you keep a capsized kayak inverted until you are ready to bail it out or get back in. A swamped kayak that is right side up is inherently unstable and susceptible to taking on more water. By keeping it upside down, you will minimize the amount of additional water that collects in the boat while maintaining an air pocket that improves buoyancy.

With these points in mind, try some swimming. Always wear a PFD and make sure that your boat is suitably equipped with flotation. Paddle out to deep water, capsize, wet exit, and surface, holding the boat by the coaming and keeping a grip on the paddle. Now swim to the bow of the inverted kayak and get hold of some solid fitting. Lifting toggles are ideal for this, but be careful of large grab loops. In rough water a swamped kayak can spin around its long axis. If your hands or fingers are in a loop when this happens, they might become trapped.

Transfer the paddle to the same hand that is holding the boat and strike out for shore using a back or side stroke. If in the process you have lost hold of the paddle, stay with the kayak and swim it and yourself to the paddle. Paddles drift very slowly, kayaks very swiftly. Also make sure when practicing, and in all future outings, that your equipment is securely stowed.

There are some paddlers who like to tie a line between the paddle and the boat or themselves. This paddle leash is intended to keep the paddle from drifting off, and leaves the hands free to work on other tasks. The idea is sound, but there is a danger that the leash can get tangled around you or the boat. So, for the sake of safety, make sure that the leash can be released from the paddle easily and that you disconnect it when in turbulent water that might capsize or spin the kayak.

EMPTYING

A kayak with water in it is more than a damp annoyance. It's unsafe. With sea water weighing 64 pounds per cubic foot and fresh water weighing 62, it doesn't take much of it to drastically reduce a kayak's ability to float. That same water, given free access to slosh around, can make a boat very unstable. It should be obvious then that you'll want to empty a swamped kayak as soon as you can.

To make life safer, and put the odds in your favor, you must be sure that your boat is fitted with adequate flotation in both ends. Secured air bags are good, bulkheads and waterproof hatches even better. Most single kayaks fitted with bulkheads take on and retain a surprisingly small amount of water in their cockpits. Kayaks with no flotation can take on surprisingly great amounts of water and are not averse to sinking. Always take along something you can use to bail the boat: a sponge, a pump, or a scoop.

If you are very close to shore, it may be a wise option to wait and empty the boat there. This is especially true if the water is very cold. Emptying a boat in deep water can take quite a bit of time, and if it's cold, you'll want to avoid hypothermia by spending as little time as possible in that water.

If the shoreline is attainable and not too rocky or rough, put the stern of the inverted kayak on land and lift the bow. If the shoreline is inhospitable, stand in the shallows with the stern in deep water and lift the bow clear. In a boat with bulkheads, most of the water will collect in the forward end of the cockpit. Empty this first. Once most of the water has drained, turn the boat over and sponge or pump out the rest.

Initially you may experience some difficulty in getting the inverted boat free from the water because of suction around the cockpit opening. To relieve this, tilt the boat on its side until the cockpit rim clears the surface, breaking the seal. With the boat still in this position, lift slowly and carefully to let as much water drain from the cockpit as possible before bringing the kayak to land. Putting the weight of a fully waterlogged boat on land can break both its back and yours.

For some boats you will have to lift and drain one end and then the other. This may have to be repeated a number of times. In all of the above situations you may need to support one side of the boat to keep the boat fully inverted while draining it. Lift with your legs, not your back.

There are a number of ways to go about emptying a boat in deep water, but one seems to be more effective and reliable than the others. With the kayak inverted, swim up next to the cockpit. While holding onto your paddle with one hand, reach under the boat with the other and grab the cockpit coaming on the opposite side. With a quick motion pull this hand toward you while pushing up on the near side with the hand holding the paddle. This will smartly flip the boat upright and, if done fast enough, bring very little water aboard. Reenter the boat using a paddle float or with the help of a companion. Bail out the remaining water and get underway.

PADDLE FLOAT REENTRY

Your first attempts to get back into the kayak after a capsize might result in a startling realization. The boat, which was a little wobbly while you were in it, has now become an unpredictable demon.

There are sea kayaks that are stable enough to allow you to climb back into them without outside help. To see if yours fits this category, try this experiment: With the boat upright and you in the water, slide up onto the aft deck facing the bow. Stay on your stomach while pulling yourself forward. When over the cockpit, sit up with both legs in the water and spread out for stability. Lower your rear onto the seat and then bring your legs in. If that doesn't work, try sliding up from the middle of the boat onto the rear deck face down, inserting both legs into the cockpit, twisting around, and then lowering yourself onto the seat. Ten to one says you won't make it.

Even if you do, don't feel too sure of yourself. What might work in calm water when you're feeling fit may not do the job when it's blowing and you're tired, and maybe even a little frightened.

Using a paddle float is the most reliable reentry method for a lone paddler attempting an unassisted rescue. In this system, a float is put on one end of the paddle while the other end is held to the boat; this creates a stability-enhancing outrigger. For those who can climb aboard in calm water, the float system is a good backup. For those whose boats are tippy, the paddle float may be your only hope of getting back into the kayak. Mind you, the paddle float is not a panacea or the ultimate rescue procedure, but it has been proved to have a high success rate in a wide variety of situations. The one place it is guaranteed to fail, and should never be attempted, is inside the surfline. Never attempt any reentry res-

cue here; instead, swim or drift to shore where you can contemplate your next move in safety.

To be effective, the paddle float reentry requires preparation. First, the boat should be set up with special rigging, then you have to be willing to practice.

To rig your kayak, you'll need a relatively flat area just behind the cockpit and a series of taut straps or strong bungee cords over this area. The objective is to firmly hold the paddle perpendicular to the boat. Another part of the rigging is a place to stow the float. When considering a location, make sure that you can get at the float easily after a capsize and that the float will not become separated from you. Most paddlers stow their floats on the aft deck under bungee cords. When doing so, tie a short line from the float to the kayak to prevent accidental loss. If your float is the inflatable kind, you might want to consider keeping it partially filled so you will only have to top it off when you are in the water.

When practicing, remember that in a real situation you will probably be doing this because all else has failed or no outside help is available. So rehearse the procedures often and in varying conditions. Develop a set routine that you can follow by numbers. Remember: practice prevents panic. Here's how it goes.

- After capsizing, right the boat. Try to keep as much water out as you can, but do not bail it out at this time. Your first goal is to get out of the water.
- Move to the downwind side of the boat and put the paddle float on one of the blades. If you are using a foam block, just slip it in place. If you are using an inflatable float, put it on the blade first, then inflate it.

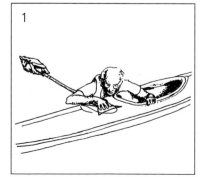

1

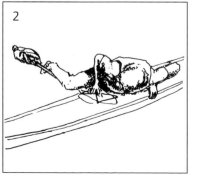

2

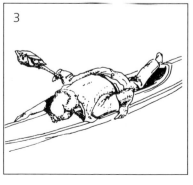

3

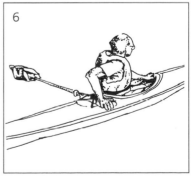

- Place the other blade under the retaining rigging on the rear deck (illustration 1, below).
- Staying forward of the paddle shaft, hoist yourself onto the aft deck with one leg resting on the paddle for support; when facing aft, this is the leg farthest from the boat. Stay face down, keep low to the boat, do not get up on your hands or elbows, and keep most of your weight on the boat, favoring the float side (illustration 2, below). Although your PFD may seem a hindrance during these contortions, do not give in to the temptation to remove it. It does provide welcome padding for your torso when crawling over the hard cockpit coaming.
- Place the leg nearest the boat into the cockpit. Maintain the face-down position, keep your weight toward the side with the float. Now put the second leg into the cockpit (illustrations 3 and 4).
- Keeping your weight toward the side with the float, rotate to face upward and slide forward onto the seat (illustrations 5 and 6).
- While keeping your weight toward the side with the float, bail out as much water as you can, put your spray skirt in place, and, if need be, pump out the rest.
- Take your paddle out of the rigging and remove the float. This can be precarious. Go slowly, cautiously, and wait for a lull in the wind or waves.

There may be times when you find yourself in a boat that is not rigged for a paddle float reentry. This does not mean that you can't use the system, only that it will be more difficult. The following procedure requires more dexterity and strength, while providing less control and stability.

After swimming around to the downwind side of the upright boat, slip the float over one of the paddle's blades, inflate it if necessary, and locate yourself aft of the cockpit. Hold the paddle shaft against the rear of the coaming with the hand closest to the cockpit. While holding the paddle in position, climb aboard the aft deck with one leg on the paddle shaft. Hoist yourself farther up onto the boat while keeping your weight toward the float side. Swing your body around and bring one leg into the cockpit and then the other. Rotate to a face-up position, slide onto the seat, and secure the boat.

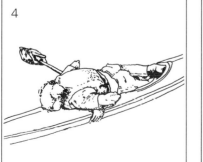

4

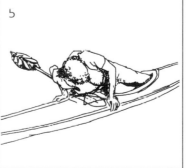

5

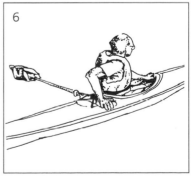

6

BOAT DYNAMICS

STABILITY

A sailboat gets stability from ballast deep below the waterline, giving it a low center of gravity. As the boat leans (heels), the ballast provides a constant righting force to keep it from capsizing.

A kayak is just the opposite. Its center of gravity is a substantial distance above the waterline. Because this is not ideal, we have to look elsewhere to get stability. And the best place we'll find it is in the movement of our bodies. This is called *dynamic stability*, and when you know how to use it, it's better than ballast.

Here's the theory: You and your kayak have a combined *center of gravity* somewhere near your waistline that is the concentration of forces pulling downward. The forces pushing upward that keep you afloat are concentrated at a spot called the *center of buoyancy*.

These two forces work against each other. But what adds spice to the equation is that while the center of gravity is always located near your belly button, the center of buoyancy changes as the boat tilts—making it variable.

When the boat is level, the center of gravity is directly above the center of buoyancy. In this condition the forces are in balance and you stay upright. If you and the boat lean over, the center of gravity and the center of buoyancy will move outward, but at different rates. As long as the upward force of the center of bouyancy is farther to the side than the downward force of the center of gravity, the boat will want to stay upright. Unfortunately you don't have to lean too far before just the opposite hap-

pens, whereupon you and your boat invert to a stable position in which you act very much like a sailboat's ballasted keel. That is, you capsize.

Capsizing is almost guaranteed if you try to hold your upper body perpendicular to the boat when it tilts. In this position the center of gravity moves rapidly to the side. To avoid this all you have to do is to hold your upper body perpendicular to the water, not the boat. This keeps your center of gravity in a more stable position closer to the boat's center of buoyancy. As the boat—the upward force—tilts one way, your upper body— the downward force—compensates and tilts the other. That's dynamic stability.

Here's how it's done: the secret is to stay loose and be able to bend sideways just above your hips. By relaxing your stomach muscles, you can separate your upper body from the boat, which is being firmly gripped by your lower body. This separation lets the boat do what it wants. It can wiggle, wobble, or flop around. As long as your upper body remains steady and upright, you'll be OK. If you let it, it happens almost automatically.

Try this. Hold your paddle horizontally in front of you. Rock the kayak by alternately lifting one knee while pushing down with the opposite buttock. Keep your body vertical. You'll see that it won't take long before you are increasing the angle of the boat far beyond what you thought would be possible. Your only limitation will be how much movement your hips and waist will allow.

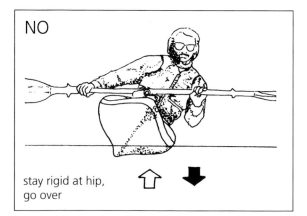

NO

stay rigid at hip, go over

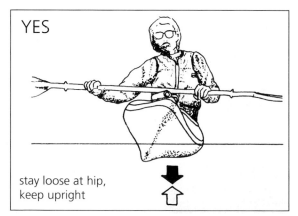

YES

stay loose at hip, keep upright

BALANCE

Although the main objective of this lesson is to explore balance, both the kayak's and yours, there will also be some side benefits. You're likely to find that you instinctively know more about kayaking than you might have thought. Unlike other lessons, this one has no right or wrong way, no musts, shoulds, or have-tos. This is about doing, not reading; about sensing, not intellectualizing. Educators may call it "discovery learning," but it's really just fooling around.

To build a foundation of confidence for the techniques that will follow, you will need to develop a feel for the natural balance of you and your boat. To do that you're going to have to get wet and, yes, have fun.

Find a place where the water's warm and protected, put on a nose clip, and make like a polar bear with a beach ball. Be careful though. If you're in a limited area such as a swimming pool, watch out for swimmers, other playing paddlers, and the sides of the pool. Be sure to stay in water at least 4 feet deep so you won't be banging your head on the bottom.

For those who have forgotten what it's like to be playful, here are some ideas on how to explore your boat's balance.

Climb into the boat from the water. First over the rear deck, then from the side. Now try to climb out of the boat. Straddle the cockpit, sit on the rear deck with your feet in the cockpit, stand up, lie down.

Try to swamp the boat completely (make sure it has flotation so it won't sink on you). You may be surprised at how little water a boat with bulkheads will take on. Now try to get into the boat from the water, and then from a dock or pool side. Paddle around in it with your hands. Now empty out half of the water and try the same things. Take particular notice of how the amount of water in the boat affects its stability and performance.

Find the point at which the boat capsizes. In the shallows (less than 1 foot) of a protected beach, tilt the boat over toward the shore, supporting yourself with your hand. Lean over a little, then a little more. You'll be surprised how far over you can go. Try it on both sides. The same can be done holding on to the side of a pool or dock.

While in the boat, try to bend over and "kiss" the water. See how low you can bend before going over.

Paddle with your hands, paddle with one hand, spin the boat around, go forward, backward, and figure out how to make it go sideways. Sit on the rear deck and paddle. If the cockpit is large enough, kneel in it and paddle.

Capsize the boat and swim underwater to bring your head up in the cockpit. Look around and see for yourself how little water collects in an upside-down kayak.

Invert the boat, crawl over it from one side to the other, and then return underwater.

Have a water fight with another paddler without using paddles. Try to fill the other boat to the point that it becomes unstable.

Become a member of the dry hair club by getting out of a capsizing boat before it goes completely over.

Experiment, make up your own games, and don't be embarrassed. The whole idea of kayaking is to have fun. And if it's any consolation to your ego, there are very few top paddlers who haven't at one time or another just fooled around with their boats. The more familiar you become with your kayak, the easier the whole learning process will be; and the more relaxed you are in your boat and on the water, the better your technique will be. So lighten up and explore the balance.

PADDLING BASICS

6

HOLDING THE PADDLE

Paddling is fundamental to, and the essence of, sea kayaking. Right from the start, you must develop a sense for a good paddle stroke and then evolve one that is right for you. This chapter covers the skills you'll need to do that; for now, be sure to read through this whole chapter several times before tackling each lesson separately; that way you'll understand the lesson sequences inherent in learning to paddle.

Your goal is to find a style that is efficient enough to carry you long distances and comfortable enough to be maintained for hours. To achieve this you will have to make many choices along the way, the first being how you hold your paddle.

To start, you must determine your effective grip range on the shaft. Where on the shaft you put your hands within that range is completely up to you. Their position affects, and is responsive to, your stroke. And, because your stroke will vary, so will the position of your hands. For maximum power to accelerate, maneuver, or push into a strong current or headwind, use a wide grip. This is like low gear on a car, giving a slower but more powerful stroke. If you bring your hands closer together, you get a higher gearing, with more blade motion for less arm movement. This is used to sustain a cruising speed or for fast traveling in calm conditions.

To shift gears effectively, you have to know the range of hand grips. You can determine the outer limits of your grip by holding the paddle over your head, making a right angle with your elbows so your forearms are vertical and your upper arms are horizontal (photo 1). This is the position for maximum low gear. Mark the shaft with tape just outside your small fingers, making sure that the marks are equal distances from the center. To find the limit for high gear, bring the shaft up to your shoulders with your upper arms against your sides (photo 2). Mark the shaft near your thumbs. Your effective grip range is between the marks. For now, pick any spot within this range that feels comfortable.

How the paddle is gripped is determined by which hand you choose as your control hand. With feathered paddles the control hand holds the shaft to allow wrist and forearm motion to produce the proper blade-to-water angle for each stroke. This hand is fixed to the shaft and never changes its grip. The other hand keeps a loose hold on the shaft, allowing it to rotate freely. Either hand can be used for control. With nonfeathered paddles both hands simultaneously perform the control function.

The control hand holds the shaft so the top edge of the nearest blade lines up with the top row of your knuckles (illustration 3). Maintain that grasp so you'll always know the angle of the blade in relation to your hand. Blade angle in relation to the water is changed by moving your wrists or forearms, not by loosening your grip and turning the shaft. Once you lose your grip, you lose your orientation to the blade; this makes knowing the blade's angle a constant guessing game.

Don't keep a death grip on the shaft, there's no need for it, and it will only bring discomfort. Hold the shaft in the curve of your fingers, with most of the gripping done by the thumb and forefinger. Keep a light and responsive hold. It may seem too delicate, but your fist will automatically tighten up when needed, so don't worry. A relaxed grip gives you a longer stroke and reduces lateral wrist movements that can stress tendons.

top of blade aligns with top knuckles of control hand

1   2   3

BASIC STROKE: NONFEATHERED

A nonfeathered paddle has its blades set parallel to one another and requires a minimum of shaft rotation. A feathered paddle has its blades offset from 60 to 90 degrees to one another and requires shaft rotation for each blade to meet the water at the desired angle. The choice between the two is subjective. The success you have with one over the other has to do with your level of comfort and the use of proper technique.

Find out which type of paddle you feel most at ease with. To do this use a take-apart paddle that lets you switch from nonfeathered to either right- or left-hand-controlled feathered. For this lesson set the blades for nonfeathered.

All paddling is a complex cycle of separate components that build on each other. Within each stroke there is a pushing and pulling of opposing arms, wrist motion, and twisting of the body (torso rotation). Start with the basic pulling motion of the arms (we'll add the important motions of your wrists and torso in subsequent lessons).

You may want to take your inaugural strokes on land or while standing in hip-deep water to add a touch of authenticity and resistance as you pull on the blade. When you're ready to try it in a boat, head for an open stretch of protected water, not a swimming pool. You'll need a lot of room to paddle so you can have time to make mistakes, correct them, and get a feel for what you are doing.

When in the boat, wedge your knees under the deck, and put light pressure on the foot braces to hold your lower back snugly against its support. Don't slouch, and do keep your head up and eyes on the horizon. Hold the paddle shaft away from you at chest height, with your arms slightly bent and your elbows pointing out and down.

You can start off on either side, but for the sake of this lesson, begin on the right. Extend your right arm so it is straight; keep your left hand held close-in, up around your shoulder. Place the blade gently in the water, making a clean entry with no splashing (illustration 1). To get a good long stroke, you'll want to set the blade in the water as far forward as possible without having to lean forward. You can extend your reach, and reduce wrist strain, by straightening your last three fingers so the shaft is momentarily being held by the thumb and forefinger. Aim for a spot near your foot and put the

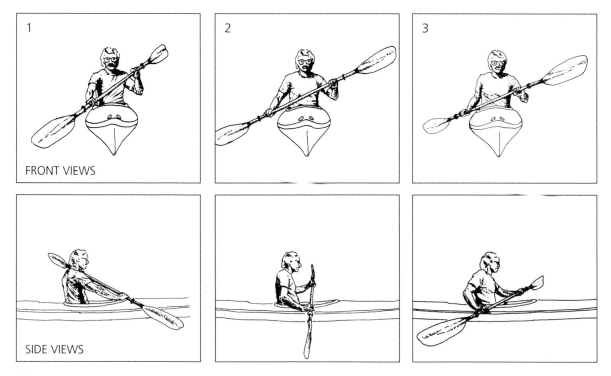

1

2

3

FRONT VIEWS

SIDE VIEWS

blade into the water close to the boat. Immerse the blade almost to the shaft but no deeper, and try to maintain this depth throughout the stroke.

To help you envision the forces involved, think of the blade as being inserted into something solid while you pull yourself and the kayak toward it. You are not pulling the blade back through the water as it might appear.

Only after the blade is completely immersed can power be applied by your right arm. As it comes back, your left hand simultaneously goes forward as if making a diagonal punch toward the bow, without crossing the centerline of the boat. The palm of the left hand faces forward with fingers relaxed. The shaft angle should be kept comfortably flat (2). This way the blade in the air is less apt to be caught by the wind, drips will not find their way to you, and the stroke will provide support as well as propulsion. Your left hand will have most of the responsibility for shaft angle. Let it go no higher than eye level.

Throughout the pull, be aware of the blade's angle to the water as seen from the side. The blade should stay close to perpendicular to the surface of the water. If the top of the blade tilts toward the bow of the kayak, the blade will want to dig deeper. If the top tilts toward the stern, the blade will want to lift out.

Maximum power should be exerted as your knees are passing the blade. Once your hips are level with the blade, the forward thrust of the stroke diminishes. This should coincide with your left hand being at the limit of its forward reach (3 and 4). So ease off on the pull and lift the blade up with a brisk slicing motion. After the blade is out, keep raising your right hand until it assumes a position similar to that for your left hand at the beginning of the stroke. This directs the left-hand blade forward and down toward the water so it is ready to start the stroke on the left side (5 and 6).

Once you've mastered the separate elements, concentrate on having a smooth, continuous action. If you think about it too much, you'll only get confused. Use your brain each time you put the blade in and take it out. Let your body fill in the rest. Hold down the pace while learning, but you can throw in an occasional sprint for excitement.

BASIC STROKE: FEATHERED

To the basic arm pull used on a nonfeathered paddle, you will now add the wrist motion needed for feathered paddling.

At this point many novices inwardly say, "Why bother with feathering now? I'll just use a nonfeathered paddle to learn the basics and make a decision between the two later." You could, but you wouldn't be giving yourself a fair chance. Because you are eventually going to have to choose, don't be tempted to stay with nonfeathering because of a preconceived notion that feathered paddling is more complex or difficult. It's not, but you'll have to prove that to yourself. Give it time, and it will soon become obvious which feels more natural. When this happens, make your decision and stick with it. From there on don't vacillate from one to the other. This will only confuse you and delay the ultimate refining of your stroke. When ambivalent, go with feathering first. If you find it's not for you, it will be easier to switch over to nonfeathering than the other way around.

Now for another choice. Which hand will be your controlling hand? The control hand uses wrist and forearm motion to rotate the shaft so that each blade meets the water at the desired angle. Its grip on the shaft remains constant so that the top edge of the nearest blade lines up with the top row of your knuckles. The other hand keeps a loose hold, acting only as a guide.

Curiously, most people, whether left- or right-handed, seem to prefer right-hand control. You'll probably know which is best for you after a few trial strokes. You've got a take-apart paddle, so experiment. But once again, you'll eventually have to pick a control hand and stick with it.

To start, it will be instructive to see what the control hand really does. Hold the paddle in front of you with your control hand properly positioned and your arms almost straight. When the control-side blade is vertical, the opposite blade should be almost horizontal. Now twist your control wrist back to bring your knuckles toward you as if giving the gas to a motorcycle. Bring your wrist far enough back so that the blades switch positions, with the control blade now being almost horizontal and the noncontrol blade vertical. Try it again, but this time bend your elbow to raise your forearm as you twist your wrist. Don't juggle the shaft around in your hands to change the blade angle. Hold the shaft

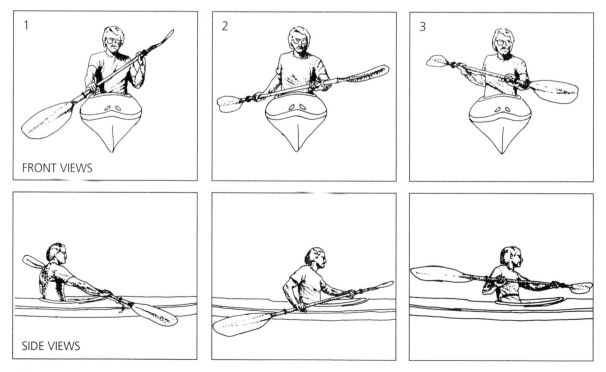

1   2   3

FRONT VIEWS

SIDE VIEWS

securely with your control hand. Let your wrist and forearm change the angle. Practice until you are confident about being able to present a vertical blade to the water on either side. See if you can do it with your eyes closed, using only the feel of your control hand.

For some reason it often seems easier to make your first stroke on the control side. So put the control-side blade into the water first and go through the same hand and arm motions as you did with the nonfeathered paddle (illustrations 1 and 2). On the control side the stroke is exactly the same until you lift the blade from the water. It is here that you begin to raise your forearm and twist the wrist back. This will bring the noncontrol blade vertical, down, forward, and ready for the stroke on the other side (3).

Put the noncontrol blade in the water and begin pulling yourself toward it while straightening the opposite arm (4 and 5). Now you can ease (but not reposition) your control-hand grip, palm facing down and forward, with fingers relaxed and wrist fairly straight.

Lift the blade out when it is opposite your hips. As you continue lifting, begin to twist the control wrist forward, while lowering and extending the forearm.

This will bring the control blade vertical, down, and forward (6). The cycle is complete and you are ready to start the stroke again on the control side.

Don't get discouraged if your beginning strokes end in disaster. Paddling takes a tremendous amount of practice before you can attain a good fluid stroke. Common problems at this stage are not using the full blade, leaning forward to extend your reach, gripping the shaft too tightly, bringing the upper hand across the centerline, and continuing the stroke beyond the hip. With all the wrist twisting and relaxing of fingers there is the possibility of losing orientation between the control hand and the blade. Check your grip occasionally to be sure.

Don't think you are a weakling because you feel beat after paddling short distances. It's not you. It's because you've only been using the relatively small muscles in your arms. No paddler is strong enough to go any distance on his or her arms alone. In the next phases of learning, you'll be adding the pushing of the opposing arm, and then the more powerful muscles of your abdomen, back, shoulder, and legs. But for now, just work on the arms and the pattern of the blade in the water.

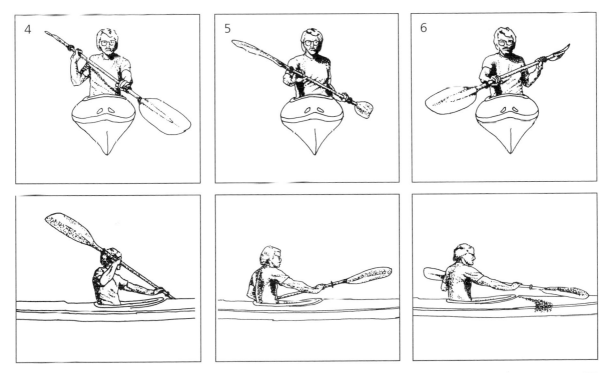

PUSH/PULL

By now you've probably managed to make the boat move by using your arms to pull it through the water. It worked, but it was hard work. That's because you were using only one arm for the job, while letting the other just guide the paddle, without putting in its fair share. Well, the free ride is over for that "other" nonpulling arm. Now you'll use it to provide a pushing force to complement the pulling arm's effort. By adding this extra power from your upper arm you'll immediately find a great strain has been taken off your pulling wrist and that paddling has become a lot easier.

The additional pushing motion is like using two hands to turn a steering wheel instead of one. If you prefer a more literal image, it might help to think of the paddle as a lever.

Envision at the start of each stroke that the blade is being inserted into something solid and that you are pulling the boat toward it. With this action you are using the paddle as a lever. Unfortunately, it is a very inefficient one, but with the addition of some pushing from the upper arm, leverage is markedly improved.

Now envision a new and more complex lever. Like all levers, it needs a pivot point, a fulcrum—your pulling hand. As before, you are trying to move an immovable blade through the water to pry the boat forward. But now, the motive forces will come from both the pulling and pushing arms.

What makes this lever complex is that your pulling hand becomes a moveable fulcrum. As it hauls the boat toward the blade, it is also acting as a pivot point for the shaft, which is being pushed forward by the upper arm. The result is a combined increase in power from the hauling of the pulling arm and the leveraged prying of the pushing arm.

However you understand it, both arms are now sharing the work. The balance isn't even; about 65 percent of the force is coming from the pulling arm and 35 percent from the pushing arm; but it's more than enough for you to be able to notice a tremendous difference in performance.

The pushing begins as soon as you start the stroke with your lower pulling arm. The two hands move in opposite directions but at similar speeds. The pushing force increases through the middle of the stroke, about where your knee passes the blade. At this point both arms are equally extended and maximum pushing power is being applied. The arms

continue the stroke with reduced force until the lower pulling hand is at the end of its stroke and the upper pushing arm is almost at the limit of its reach. The total motion of the pushing arm is like a slow, forward punch coming from your shoulder toward the centerline at the bow.

There is a tendency to get overenthusiastic about pushing. Some paddlers may complete the push way before the pull has finished or apply maximum push before the pull has even started. While learning, keep your pace down, and use gentle pressure so you can feel the pushing and pulling and where the two change places.

Bringing the pushing hand above eye level, dropping it near the end of the stroke, crossing the boat's centerline, or holding the shaft too close to your chest will all limit the success of your pushing. Don't develop a death grip with your upper hand. Keep your fingers relaxed and slightly open, with the web between the thumb and index finger taking most of the pressure (this also helps to keep the wrist straight).

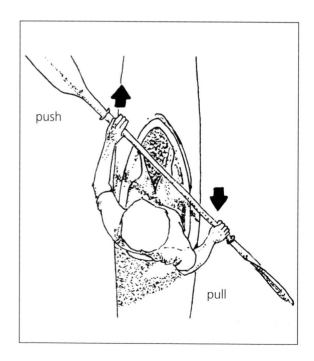

push

pull

BODY TWIST

Put your back into it! As well you should, because the more (and the larger the) muscles you can enlist to help, the easier the job becomes.

If you've ever used a handsaw, you probably figured out that rather than just sawing back and forth with your arms, the more efficient way was to move your shoulders and put the muscle and momentum of your body into it. You got farther faster and with less effort. It's the same with paddling. To get the full range of motion and the benefit of the muscles in your abdomen, back, and shoulders, you will have to sit upright without slouching or leaning back. And even more than before, you'll need to be well-braced in the kayak. Your feet, legs, and hips should be at one with the boat, while you are free to move from the waist up.

The stroke begins as before, with one arm extended ahead and the other bent and close to your body. To this you add body twist by swinging the shoulder of the extended arm forward. No need to go into contortions, just a comfortable rotation of the torso without straining the waist or back.

This position sets up your body to recoil with full power. It also increases your reach so you can put the blade in farther forward, extending the useful length of your stroke.

The releasing of the collective body power that rotates the shoulder begins when the pulling arm starts the stroke. This release has a multiple effect. As your pulling shoulder comes back, the shoulder on the pushing side is going forward. Both the pulling and pushing components of your stroke are being augmented.

During the stroke's maximum power phase, almost all the paddling force is coming from your torso, with the least from your pushing arm, and the remainder supplied by the pulling arm. The body's motion is not a jerk or a snatch, but a smooth uncoiling of a powerful spring. By keeping your arms slightly bent and away from your chest, you will get the full use of this power. You can also help, and it might even come naturally, by pressing the foot brace on the stroke side. This is a reflexive action that helps to push the kayak forward. As you take a stroke on the right side, press on the right foot brace; as you stroke on the left, press on the left.

When the blade is withdrawn at the end of the stroke, both the pulling and pushing shoulders will have followed through an almost-90-degree swing.

The pulling shoulder is now pointing back, and the pushing shoulder is now close to the same angle as your pulling shoulder was at the beginning of the stroke. This sets you up to start on the other side.

An interesting experiment is to restrict arm motion by keeping both arms locked, using only body twist to do the work. You might surprise yourself with your own power. You can also play at seeing how far you can exaggerate the twisting. Try accelerating from a dead stop to see which muscles are really being used. You should feel it in your abdomen, as if you were doing sit-ups, and in your legs from pushing on the foot braces. At first your legs and abdomen may ache, but as your muscles strengthen with practice, this will go away. The more you incorporate body twist into your stroke, the more the soreness of unused muscles leaves the arms for the shoulders and abdomen. Eventually even this gives way to a stroke that feels effortless.

Although body twist should be used as much as possible, you need not go to extremes. For most paddling, only gentle forces need be applied with small amounts of rotation. Only when confronted with strong winds or currents will you need to really coil up and unwind the body's full power.

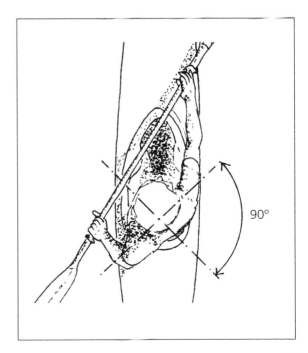

THE COMPLETE STROKE

There are very few absolutes when it comes to paddling; what standards there are have been presented. Take them only as a foundation, something from which you can build a style that is uniquely your own. From here on you should strive to develop a stroke that is both powerful and comfortable.

To do this, you will have to relinquish the idea of separate wrist, arm, and body motions. Your goal is a fluid stroke. The best way to achieve this is through practice; and that means constant practice for long stretches at a time. While training, try not to think the stroke through. Let it happen on its own, and when you feel it's right, put your brain in gear to watch what you're doing. Don't be discouraged if it takes time. And once in a while go back to working on the fundamental components, just to make sure you aren't sacrificing a small part for the sake of the total package.

Dos and Don'ts

Here is a quick review of things you should *do* while practicing:

- Keep the power blade fully immersed and perpendicular to the water.
- Keep the alignment between the controlling hand and the nearest blade constant.
- Position your grip on the shaft and keep it loose.
- Sit upright with your head steady and eyes on the horizon.
- Hold the shaft away from your chest with your elbows slightly bent. Place the blade as far ahead as possible at the beginning of the stroke without bending forward at the waist. Bring your shoulder forward to increase your reach.
- Put the blade into the water close to the boat and cleanly so there is no splash.

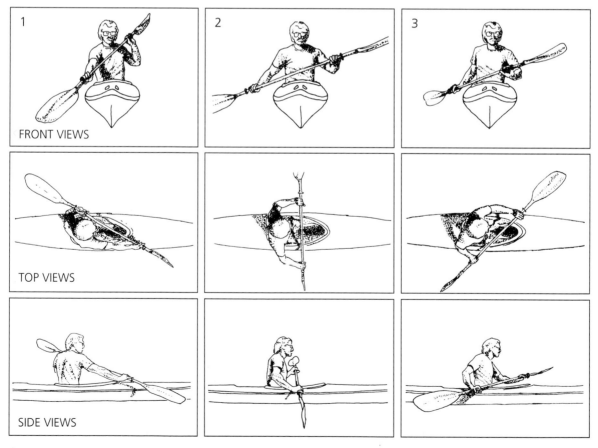

1

2

3

FRONT VIEWS

TOP VIEWS

SIDE VIEWS

- Use the palm of the upper hand to push, guided by slightly opened fingers.
- Maintain a shaft angle that is as shallow as practical.
- Pull and push with a steady, even pressure that favors the pulling side.
- Get the majority of your power from your torso, then the pulling arm, and least of all from the pushing arm.
- Twist your torso and rotate your shoulders to pull one arm back while driving the other arm forward.
- Push against the foot brace on the pulling side.
- Apply maximum power in mid-stroke, usually as your knees are passing the blade.
- Slice the blade up and out cleanly when your hip passes it.
- Avoid unnecessary force.

Here is a quick review of things you *don't* want to do while practicing:

- Slouch or lean back in the seat.
- Hold your arms close to the chest.
- Allow the pushing hand to go above eye level or across the centerline of the boat.
- Keep too tight a grip on the shaft.
- Juggle your grip to change the blade's angle to the water.
- Paddle using only your arms.
- Raise the upper blade high in the air, where it can catch wind and drip water on you.
- Apply power before the blade is fully immersed.
- Continue the stroke far beyond your hips.
- Lean back and forth, or rock side to side, as you paddle.

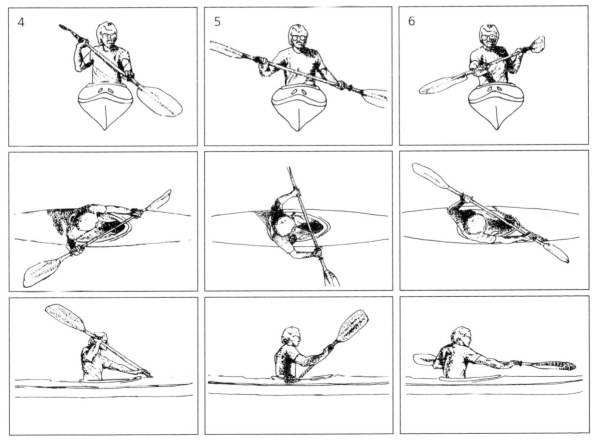

STOPPING AND BACKING

Although forward progress is always desirable, there are times when a hasty retreat will be prudent if not life-saving. In addition to general maneuvering, backing can be used as a holding action when you are caught in a current, giving you time to contemplate your next move, or to keep you in position on the back of a breaking wave. But before going backward, it is worthwhile to first look into the techniques of stopping.

A kayak's maximum speed is not likely to exceed 5 mph, yet its momentum can come as quite a shock when you attempt to stop. Because a lot of effort and balance are needed to do this, it will be best not to try to stop with one Herculean stroke.

When you decide to stop, hold the shaft low and near your body with your elbows tucked in. Have the blade slightly behind your hip and maintain a vertical, or slightly forward-leaning, blade angle. Immerse one blade for a second or two, and then the other. Your arms should stay flexible, pushing forward slightly, while your body twists to absorb most of the energy. Do not change your grip on the shaft in order to turn the power face frontward. In doing so you risk losing your hand's orientation to the blade; the resistance of the back of the blade will be more than enough. To stop in a straight line, try to provide an even braking force by not keeping one blade in longer than the other. Three or four quick jabs on alternate sides should do it.

The forces absorbed with body twist in stopping will be reinvested in the backstroke, for its power comes almost exclusively from the torso. Position yourself in the boat so you are sitting upright or leaning back slightly, making sure that your seat and lower back are locked in place to take the transmitted force. As with stopping, your grip is never changed and only the back side of the blade is used.

The starting position is with the body fully rotated and the paddle held almost parallel to the side of the boat. The blade is put into the water about 2 feet behind the hips, with the arms and elbows close to the body. You then unwind (rotate) forward bringing your arms and the paddle with you while leaning back to put your weight behind the stroke. Some pushing with the palm, keeping your fingers relaxed, may be incorporated to help direct the blade. Maximum power is used as the hips pass, and the blade is lifted up and out as the knees pass.

To get the most power from your backstroke, hold the shaft so that the full back of the blade touches the water as it enters. The paddle is kept as vertical and parallel to the side of the boat as possible throughout the stroke, with power being exerted down and forward. A less powerful stroke, but one with more steering ability, can be done by slipping the blade in edge first and making the stroke a broad sweep. Power here is exerted out and forward. The typical backing stroke will be somewhere between these two extremes, varying to hold the desired course.

The faster you paddle backward, the harder it is to steer. So paddle slowly, making adjustments in your stroke as you go. Balance may also prove difficult. Looking over one shoulder and then the other is sure to disorient you. So pick one, and keep your eyes on a fixed point of reference. If any distances are involved, you need only give an occasional look over that one shoulder, or use a reference point off your bow to guide you.

STOPPING

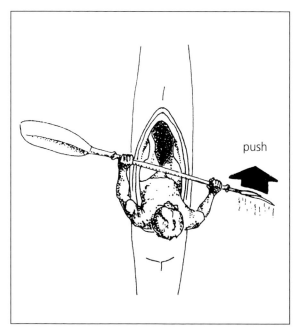

push

BACKING

1 start

2 push through

3 end stroke

4 change sides

61

FINE POINTS OF PADDLING BASICS

Feathered vs. Nonfeathered. You need no other reason to choose one style of paddling over the other than a simple "it works for me." Even so, it does seem a paradox. How can one be just as good as the other if they are so different? Maybe a little bit of history will clarify the matter.

For centuries the Eskimos used relatively long paddles with narrow nonfeathered blades. These were perfect for traveling great distances at a constant speed, easy to control in high winds, and unequaled for the intended job.

Then, around the middle of the 1800s, the kayak was introduced to "civilization" and put to uses other than those for which it was originally designed. The turn-of-the-century sportsman was more interested in increasing the power of the stroke for quicker spurts than in long-range endurance, so a completely different paddle was devised. This new paddle used bigger blades for more power, and was shorter for a more rapid stroke. It also did the job it was intended to do, except for one problem. When paddling into a headwind it took a lot of effort to push that big blade through the air on the return stroke. To alleviate this, someone set the blades at opposing angles (feathered). Now the returning blade went through the air horizontally, so its size was no longer a problem. Thus, feathering was born, and has stayed on. Just for the record, here's what the experts say about each.

The main advantage to the nonfeathered style is that it is supposedly easier on the wrists and forearms, although poor technique can negate this advantage. The drawback is that with larger modern blades there is more resistance when paddling into the wind. An advantage is that paddle control is easier when the wind is from the side. The combined arm and upper body movements are simpler, but seem awkward to some. There may be a mechanical advantage to feathering because it allows more powerful upper body rotation. Proper technique will reduce strain to the wrist and forearm of the control hand. There is less resistance while paddling into a headwind, although strong side winds make controlling the paddle harder. The wrist, arm, and upper body movements take more time to get used to, but feel quite natural once mastered.

So you see there is no answer. Try both. Give each a fair chance. Pick one, and then stick with it.

Practice good technique for whichever method you choose. Always do warm-up exercises before paddling (see part 3, Graduate Courses, Body Basics, for suggested exercises).

Refining Wrist Position. No matter which style of paddling you choose, be aware of the position of your wrists in relation to your forearms. Try to maintain a neutral wrist position, which is the relationship that your forearm, wrist, and hand fall into when they hang at your side. In this neutral position the wrist is relaxed, and there is minimal wear and strain on the interconnecting tendons. One of the best ways of ensuring this is to keep a loose, open grip on the shaft. This means pushing primarily with the palm near the thumb and forefinger while keeping your fingers relaxed, and beginning the pulling stroke with the last three fingers extended and the shaft cradled between your thumb and forefinger. In addition, a loose grip also improves blood circulation and hand warmth, and reduces the likelihood of tendonitis (inflamed tendons) or blisters. Keeping your hands dry can also prevent blisters. Do this with drip rings and by paddling with a low shaft angle.

Different Strokes. The forward stroke is remarkably variable. Strokes during which the paddle is nearly vertical, passing close to the hull and parallel to the centerline, have the most propulsive and the least turning or supporting effect. This is your power or racing stroke. It provides maximum drive, but offers little lateral support or steering moment.

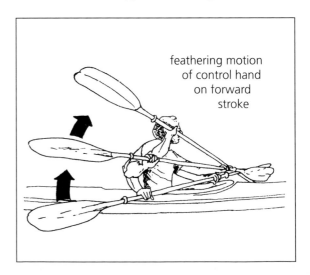

feathering motion
of control hand
on forward
stroke

Strokes during which the paddle is held at a low angle, so it makes a broad sweeping arc, have less propulsive but more turning or supporting effect. This is your control stroke. It provides plenty of lateral support and steering moment, but offers less drive. Between these extremes you will be able to find strokes that propel the kayak at a good speed for long distances with adequate steering control through a wide variety of sea conditions.

In addition to the basic propulsion strokes, you will learn others that can turn the kayak or aid in stability. None is a separate entity, and all should be linked together. This linking of strokes provides an economy of effort that allows you to exert less power to achieve the same results with fewer strokes. Keep this in mind as your repertoire of maneuvers increases.

Keeping the Boat Going in a Straight Line. If you find that the boat won't go straight when you want it to, try paddling slowly and thoughtfully at first. Many novices paddle too vigorously at the expense of good control. They wind up being unable to hold a course and wander all over the place. The more force you put into a stroke, the more perfect it must be. So go easy. And don't rush it either. A reasonable cruising cadence is about 3 seconds for a complete cycle. But this can vary according to the type of paddle and conditions.

An inability to maintain a straight course can also come from uneven leverage on the shaft. Everyone has one arm that is stronger than the other. If this is not kept in check, you'll have a more powerful stroke on your stronger side. Another cause is that your grip might shift. To prevent this, use tape to mark reference points on the shaft.

Don't rock the boat. Literally. Don't lean forward when you put the blade in, and don't lean back when you take it out. The bobbing created by this back-and-forth motion wastes energy and slows down the kayak. Side-to-side rocking comes from shifting your weight and leaning over with each stroke. This too is wasteful.

Your blade is not a windmill making great arcs in the sky. Seen from the side, the tip of each blade makes an oval rather than a circular path during its cycle.

In the beginning it's all right and probably necessary to watch each blade's path through the water, your hands on the shaft, and all the rest that is new. Continue doing this only until you've got a sense for where each blade is during the cycle. From then on start keeping your head up. Find a landmark in the distance and go for it. This will help you steer with small corrective adjustments in your stroke and learn to understand what you are doing by feel, not sight.

You might find that the "perfect" stroke as described here may not work for you. And that's OK. Everyone has an individual style that incorporates at least some of these elements. Do what you can to get close, while at the same time working within the limitations of your own body. You are not a machine.

Breathe! Don't forget to breathe. If you concentrate too hard while practicing your strokes you may not breathe at regular intervals and only make it a short distance before getting out of breath. Try to keep your head up, inhale at the beginning of a stroke on one side, and exhale at the beginning of a stroke on the other. Develop a rhythm. Relaxation during the stoke is also important. If you're tense and putting out 100 percent effort all the time, you'll collapse after a mile. Ease up, and take a split second off in the transition period between strokes.

MANEUVERING

7

FORWARD SWEEP

The forward sweep is the most fundamental of all turning strokes and seems to come almost intuitively. It's obvious: make a broad sweeping stroke on one side and the boat turns to the other. Use it while standing still to turn the boat within a small area, or use it when underway as a variation of the forward stroke for course alterations.

The forces involved are similar to those of the forward stroke. You put the blade in the water near the bow and from then on consider it as being inserted into something solid. The motion is a swing through almost half a circle. For the first part of the sweep you are pushing the bow away from the blade. During the middle part, a forward motion is imparted to the boat. And for the last part of the sweep, you are pulling the stern toward the blade.

To begin, hold the paddle in front of you. Then, without changing your grip on the shaft, move your arms and the paddle out toward the side on which you will sweep. The sweeping arm should be almost straight and the hand of the other arm should rest near your body over the boat's centerline.

In this extended position, rotate your shoulders to bring the blade as far forward as possible. Put the blade into the water so it is fully immersed, maintain an open grip, and lean slightly forward. Holding the paddle shaft as close to horizontal as you can, use the twisting of your body to swing it in a low, broad sweep. To help move the boat, press forward on the footrest of the sweeping side with your foot and to the side with your knee or thigh. Throughout most of the stroke think of your arms, shoulders, and the paddle shaft as being locked in place and pivoting around the axis of your body, the spine. Power should come almost exclusively from the unwinding of your body, with some arm pull to help guide the blade. Only toward the last third of the stroke will the other arm push out a little to help pull your hips to the paddle and bring the stroke through its full arc.

Just before the blade reaches the boat, bend the elbow of the sweeping arm to pull it up. Try not to turn the blade's power face up at the end of the stroke. This only lifts water and wastes energy.

A sweep stroke while underway works in a somewhat different manner because the water moving past the boat begins to carry the blade aft as soon as

it is put in. The beginning part of the sweep has some turning and propulsive components, the middle part some turning and a lot of propulsive components, and the last part of the sweep has a great amount of turning and almost no propulsive components. Keep these factors in mind as you adjust your course.

Because sea kayaks are designed to travel in a straight line, it takes a lot of work to turn them. But don't overdo it. If you are dragging the blade through the water with a lot of fuss and turbulence, ease up. All you are doing is aerating the ocean, because you are causing your blade to slip rather than push or pull the boat around. The best way to improve the boat's turning ability is to reduce its underwater length by leaning it on its side. Tilt the boat only slightly toward the side of the stroke by pushing up with your knee on the opposite side from the sweep.

Another way to improve turning ability is to extend the paddle out even farther. To do this, place the sweeping hand near the center of the shaft and the other hand by the throat of the nonsweeping blade. This makes a longer lever arm, but it is not without some risks. By moving your hands you lose orientation to the blades, which may leave you momentarily vulnerable as you get reorganized for another stroke. Try to maintain the same grip for almost all maneuvers.

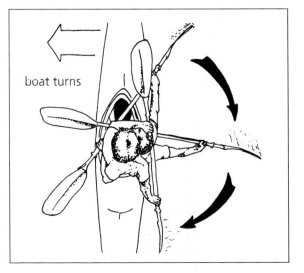

boat turns

REVERSE SWEEP

Reverse sweeps are very useful when sudden changes of direction and braking are needed. There's not a whole lot of difference between a forward and a reverse sweep. But what there is, is important.

The main difference is power from the body. What you give up for power is stability. Because your body is centered directly over the paddle at the beginning of the stroke, your center of gravity is higher and you are not as solidly rooted as with other strokes.

Most everything else is very much like a forward sweep done backward. The hand, arm, body, and paddle positions are the same. Blade positions, too, do not change, although the stroke is made using the back of the blade, not the power face. While sitting upright, you rotate your body and reach as far back as you can, keeping the sweeping arm straight. Hold the paddle shaft as close to horizontal as possible and swing forward in a low broad arc while pushing yourself back with the foot on the sweep side. Apply the greatest force in the more effective first third of the sweep. Almost all power should come from the twisting of your body, with some pushing of the sweeping arm for guidance and pulling from the other arm near the end of the stroke. At the completion of the arc, withdraw the blade sharply before you hit the side of the kayak. You might also want to lean forward at the end, adding a little extra power to what would normally be a weak position.

While standing still, you can spin the boat within its own length by alternating forward and reverse sweeps on opposite sides. While moving, the first third of the reverse stroke is a powerful way to steer. And when combined with other strokes, such as the stern rudder or low brace (which are also described in this section), it becomes part of the most powerful steering combination available.

Both the forward and reverse sweeps, like the forward paddling stroke, can be linked with other strokes. Go for smooth transitions and economy of motion.

STERN RUDDER STROKE

The stern rudder stroke is not a stroke in the strictest sense of the word. You do not place the blade in the water and actively push or pull the kayak around it. It is more of a passive action, in which the flow of water past the kayak is deflected to induce a turn. The result is precise control without losing too much boat speed. It can be used for fine course corrections while paddling, in tight spots where wide sweeping strokes won't work, or for sharp turns when considerable momentum has been built up such as in going downwind or sliding down the face of a wave.

To steer with the stern rudder, rotate your body and trail the blade on the side you wish to turn to as if setting up for a reverse sweep. The arm farthest back, which takes the force of the steering, is kept almost straight, with the other bent and held near the body. The blade is fully immersed, perpendicular in relation to the water, and set off at a shallow angle from the centerline of the boat, about a foot away, with the back of the blade facing out. By simply holding the blade you will immediately cause the boat to turn to the side that the blade is on. By adding a pushing resistance, not a sweep, you can tighten the turn.

Holding the paddle away from and nearly parallel to the boat can have more versatility. In this way you can make turns in either direction. Slightly less powerful turns can be made as before by pushing the blade away from the boat. Turns toward the opposite direction, but with considerably less range and dramatic results, can be made by pulling the blade toward the boat.

In any situation, too much pushing or pulling resistance will ultimately slow the boat. This affects turning ability because the power of the stern rudder is directly related to the speed of the boat through the water. The faster the kayak is going, the more responsive it is to rudder motion.

There are refinements that can be added to the stern rudder stroke to improve its utility and effectiveness. By rolling your wrist you can change the angle of the blade to the water and improve its worth as a deflecting vane. Just tilt the top of the blade toward the direction you would like to turn. This can be used on its own with the blade held in one position for ultradelicate course changes, or it can be used in conjunction with a pushed or pulled stern rudder to augment the effect. Another refine-

ment is to use the paddle as a tiller. The rear hand stays in place and the forward hand pushes or pulls the shaft to act like the tiller on a sailboat. In theory, the "tiller" acts as a lever to put greater effort into a turn.

The stern rudder stroke is rarely used on its own. Most often it is part of a series of strokes. For instance it works well when added to the end of a forward stroke, which is convenient because you have to be moving at a fair clip to use the stern rudder stroke anyway. It also links up with or converts easily into the beginnings of a reverse sweep or a low brace. Try combinations so you can flow from one stroke to another, making a continuous maneuver out of separate elements.

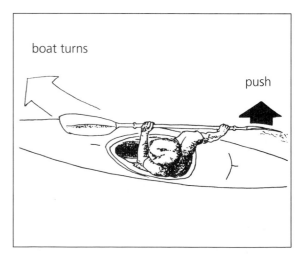

boat turns

push

The rudder is a relatively recent advance in marine engineering. For centuries, vessels were steered by a stern rudder stroke from a paddle; later the paddle was lashed to one side of a pointed stern. About 1200 A.D., this steering board (from which we got the word *starboard*) arrangement was replaced by the rudder. For larger vessels there is no more efficient steering device.

Rudders for kayaks have proved to be both a convenience and a disadvantage. Today most manufacturers outfit sea kayaks with rudders or offer them as an add-on accessory. The contemporary kayak rudder is tough, dependable, and ideally suited to controlling weathercocking, which is the turning of the boat into the wind in response to wind blowing from the side.

Almost all kayaks are prone to some level of weathercocking. This makes holding a course across or away from the wind difficult. A rudder counteracts this tendency by allowing all paddling energy to be put into propulsion rather than steering. This is where the rudder is a boon.

The disadvantage is in what you give up for the convenience. What you sacrifice with most rudder systems is the loss of a firm foot brace. In some systems the foot pedals lock in place when not in use, but once the rudder is engaged, the pedals move and solid bracing is lost. Other systems cannot be locked at all. With these systems your only option is to brace your heels on the bottom of the boat and push against them. Another system uses pivoting foot pads that combine some solid bracing with steering.

Almost all rudders are foot-controlled. Press on the right pedal and the boat turns right; left pedal, left turn. Compared with the stern rudder stroke, a rudder produces little drag, which means that it barely slows the boat. However, a rudder does not turn a kayak as quickly as a sweep stroke used in conjunction with edging (see page 87).

A rudder should be used gently. You should never throw it way over to one side to start a turn; this is called *oversteering*, and it only creates drag. Make minor corrections, watch the bow swing, and before the bow is pointing where you would like, bring the rudder back to center. Don't wait until you need to make large corrections; make constant small corrections with subtle rudder movements. When paddling in waves or a steady wind from one direction, set the rudder at a constant minimal angle. Don't try to adjust your course for every wave that yaws you one way and then the next. You'll impede the boat's progress and eventually drive yourself nuts. Keeping within 10 degrees of a course is just fine.

Rudders are susceptible to breakage, usually when you need them most. They are particularly vulnerable in the surf, around rocks, and in shallows. Rudders are wonderful things, but don't get too dependent on them. If your boat is not too sensitive to the wind, rely on your paddling ability; a rudder can never replace this. If your boat needs a rudder, use it as a way of making life easier. Keep it cocked up until needed and then use it sparingly.

Some boats come with a skeg instead of a rudder. A skeg is like a centerboard on a sailboat. It fits into a slot near the stern and can be raised or lowered with a cable. Unlike a rudder, a skeg does not pivot and so only aids straight-line tracking, which is helpful in countering weathercocking. In rough water, a rudder often loses contact with the water when the stern pops up over the trough of a wave; skegs are less prone to do this, and thus keep you on track better in heavy seas. With a skeg-equipped boat, turning is left to the skill of the paddler.

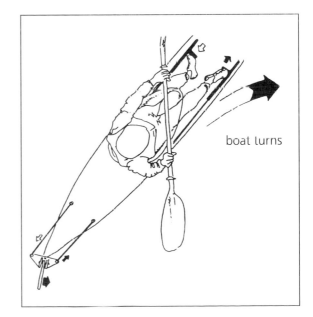

boat turns

DRAW STROKE

The kayak is one of the few vessels that can be made to travel sideways with any sort of control. This comes in very handy for maneuvering around obstacles, rafting up with others, and positioning yourself to aid in a rescue.

When moving to the side, you should use a draw stroke for strong bursts of power to cover short distances in a hurry. It is simple and direct. You place your blade in the water and then haul the boat toward it.

To set up for the stroke, hold the paddle in the forward-paddling grip and turn your body to the side. Reach out and bring the shaft almost to vertical with the power face of the blade inward. Put the blade into the water 2 to 3 feet from the boat directly opposite your hips and immersed almost to the shaft. The lower arm will be straight and the upper one bent about 90 degrees.

The main action of the stroke is a pull from the lower arm at about waist height. Most of the power comes from this arm, with only a small amount from the upper arm adding some pushing motion. As you pull, the boat will have a tendency to lean into the stroke, hindering its ability to slip over the water. With a gentle stroke this will be of no concern, but if you're putting some power into it, you'll want to level the boat by pushing up with your knee on the stroke side.

Do not let the blade get under the kayak. When about a foot from the blade, twist your lower wrist so the shaft rotates 90 degrees, causing the power face to look aft. When set like this, the blade can be knifed back up through the water to the set-up position, from which you can straighten your wrist and draw the paddle back in again. To end the stroke, or if you are having trouble changing blade angle, the blade can be lifted clear of the water. At the end of the draw bring your upper arm forward and your lower arm back. This will slice the blade up and out. From here you can proceed into something else (such as a reverse sweep) or begin the draw once again.

During successive strokes you'll find that one end of the boat advances more quickly than the other. To correct this, start your pull closer to the end that is lagging behind.

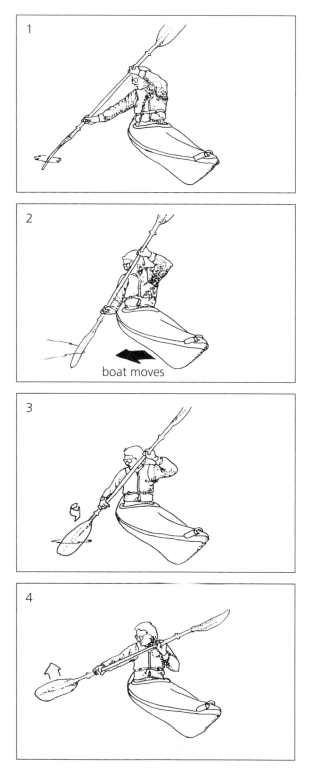

1

2

boat moves

3

4

SCULLING DRAW

The sculling draw stroke provides a constant pull that moves the kayak sideways. It won't give you the draw stroke's bursts of power and it requires a bit of finesse, but because there is no recovery phase, you get an uninterrupted motion that is easier to control and there is less chance of being caught off balance.

Sculling is a continuous movement rather than a single stroke. By slicing an angled blade through the water, you create an action that is very similar to that of a slow-moving propeller. The resultant force can be used to pull the boat sideways through the water.

To get a feel for this force, try an experiment. Stand in hip-deep water, hold the paddle vertical, and move it back and forth through the water. If the blade is held broadside to the motion, as it would be when you are paddling, you'll feel yourself being forced forward and back. But if the blade is held at an angle to the motion, you'll feel a pulling or pushing force to the side. Play at this long enough and you'll notice that the direction of the lateral force is related to the blade's angle, which is determined by its leading edge. If the edge closest to you is leading, the paddle will be pushing inward. If the edge farthest from you is leading the motion, the paddle will pull away. This pulling effect is the basic principle of sculling.

The starting position is almost the same as that for the draw stroke: normal forward-paddling grip, body turned, shaft almost vertical, blade well-immersed with the power face in and placed about 2 feet from the boat. The lower arm will provide all the power and is kept bent throughout the stroke. The upper arm is held high and arched slightly, providing a pivot for the shaft. In this position, your upper wrist might seem awkwardly twisted, but do not change to an underhand grip. You may not have the time or presence of mind to change back in an emergency.

Turn the blade so that one of its edges is angled away from the boat approximately 30 degrees from the centerline. The paddle's motion will be in the direction of this edge and will cause the blade to pull away from the boat. By resisting this force, you transmit the pull to the kayak and follow the blade sideways.

The angled blade, power face first, is sliced forward about 4 feet. At the end of its travel, the blade angle is reversed and the paddle sliced aft, power face first, for the same distance. Blade-angle switching is done as in feathering, with a quick twist of the control hand's wrist. The control hand always directs the angle. This is so regardless of whether the control hand is in the upper or lower position. The cycle should be smooth and feel continuous; there should be no stopping where blade angles switch.

Seen from above, the paddle is pulled back and forth in a path that is parallel to the boat's centerline at a constant distance from the hull. As with the draw stroke, you may find that one end of the boat advances more quickly than the other. To correct this, shift your pull toward the end that is lagging behind. You may also need to push up with your knee on the sculling side to keep the boat from leaning into the stroke and hindering side-slip.

A tricky adaptation of the sculling draw is to do it backward. Go through the movements in the same way, except use the back of the blade with the edge closest to you leading the motion. This will push the paddle toward the boat, instead of pulling it away. Use this to get an extra touch of control without having to change sculling sides.

LINKING STROKES

Every dance instructor knows that you can learn all the steps in the world, but if you can't put them together, it ain't dancin' and you might as well not even bother going out on the floor. Dancing over the waves is the same. You can learn all the strokes, but if you can't link them together, it ain't kayaking and you had better think twice about heading off into the sunset.

In addition to the basic propulsion and maneuvering strokes, there are others that enhance stability. Each one is unique, with traits and nuances that must be learned on their own. Yet none of these strokes is intended to exist as a separate entity; they must be integrated, or linked, together.

The objective of this linking is an improved economy of effort, allowing you to exert less power to achieve the same results with fewer strokes and to respond without hesitation to changes in waves and wind. That's the goal, but even before getting to that point, you can begin to benefit from stroke-linking right now, during the learning process. Not only are most strokes intended to work together, they are also interrelated in technique. For instance, the stern rudder, reverse sweep, and sweeping low brace strokes (which you will soon learn) all have common elements. If you understand one, that information can be transposed to the others. By linking the strokes—using them together—you find these common elements and expand your capabilities.

As your repertoire of strokes increases, experiment with paddling through trial and, just as importantly, error. Try combinations; see how they join up. Work toward flowing from one stroke to another, making a continuous maneuver out of separate elements. Go for smooth transitions and minimal amounts of extraneous motion. At the same time try to develop what has been called *paddle awareness*, or knowing where your paddle and

blades are at all times without having to look at them. This requires that you maintain a constant and uniform grip with your control hand. The closer it comes to being instinctive, the more you will enjoy paddling and feel at home in your kayak. You can't react properly without this awareness. Very often there are situations in which there is no time to stop and figure out what's going on. You'll only be able to react.

Drills

To give you some idea of what is meant by linked strokes and at the same time offer practice routines, here are a few ways in which the strokes you have learned so far can be joined together.

Sweeps. Paddle forward; on one right-hand stroke convert to a forward sweep; then to a reverse sweep on the left side; the boat will turn sharply to the left; leave the blade in the water after the reverse sweep and begin in the new direction with a forward stroke.

Sideways. Do two draw strokes; at the end of the last draw change to a sculling stroke; at the end of a forward slice convert to a forward stroke; gather speed and position the blade for a lateral shift.

Backward. Paddle backward over a twisting course; make a sudden stop; turn in place using forward and reverse sweeps so you are pointing in the opposite direction; paddle back through the same twisting course.

As you can imagine, the variations are endless. Make up your own slalom course with strokes for going forward, backward, sideways, turning, and, later on, bracing. Vary from one side to the next and practice these combinations as you would individual strokes.

BRACING

8

PRINCIPLES

Sea kayaking isn't yachting, it's a water sport, and every once in a while you can expect to get wet or maybe even knocked over. But that's all part of it, as are the skills of staying upright and knowing how to keep going when it gets rough. These skills are basic to the sport and are encompassed in a group of strokes known as *braces*.

Bracing strokes can be used for recovery or support. A recovery stroke brings you upright from an unstable position, whereas a support stroke holds you in a stable one. Combine them with good balance, a strong forward stroke, and the ability to maneuver, and you and your kayak become an impressively seaworthy unit.

The feeling of self-assurance that comes with dependable bracing is fantastic, and it's a big part of the fascination most paddlers have with the sport. But you'll never know this until your bracing skills become something you can trust implicitly. Once attained, your whole approach to sea kayaking will be different. A lot of the worries and most of the fears will be gone, replaced with a new sense of confidence. You'll be able to extend your limits and finally begin to evolve a style that is uniquely yours.

At the start, bracing seems a little unnatural. Normally when you feel yourself losing balance and there is nothing to stop you, you lean the other way. In a kayak where there is obviously nothing that is going to keep you from going over, it is understandable that you would also try to do the same thing. But this is just what you should not do. The proper response is to reach out to the one thing that seems least likely to be of any help, the water.

At 800 times the density of air and virtually incompressible, water can feel very solid indeed. Remember those painful belly-flop dives when you were a kid and how unyielding the water felt? Well, one bracing stroke uses that very same principle.

And remember sticking your hand out the car window to play airplane? With your hand level you'd fly along; but if you angled it up you'd take off. Now think of something as dense as water and "flying" something even bigger than your hand through it, such as a paddle blade. It doesn't take a rocket scientist to figure out that a moving blade just might be able to support quite a lot of

weight, keeping you and your kayak from going over.

Without getting into the fluid dynamics of stalled foils, it's sufficient to understand that if the forward edge of a blade in motion is kept at a climbing angle, you'll get lift. This works whether the blade is being moved through the water or held stationary with the water moving. It also works below the surface as well as on it. And the larger the blade or the faster the water, the more lift you get.

Try standing in hip-deep water and swinging the paddle around so it skims the surface. Make it plane like a water ski and really lean on it to see how much weight it can take. You'll be surprised.

A more practical application is to incorporate that lift into your forward paddling stroke by angling the blade back slightly. This gives both propulsion and support and is a very subtle example of linking strokes.

When practicing, gradually increase the pressure you put on the paddle until you've proved to yourself that bracing works. From then on, don't hold back; be willing to commit yourself to your skill. Even though you may capsize a few times, in the end you will have to depend on your ability to brace, so keep trying. A solid paddle float may be helpful while learning, providing both flotation and a flat planing surface. You and your boat must work as one, so if you haven't already fine-tuned the fit of your boat, do so before you attempt bracing (see Making It Fit in the section Meet Your Kayak).

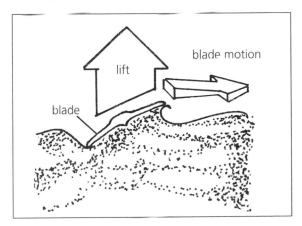

SLAP BRACE

A slap brace is a recovery stroke, something you do when you're caught off balance just as you're saying "oops." It's a way of catching yourself before going over.

The premise is simple and almost instinctive. You only have to believe that, for a split-second, water can be solid. Once you accept this, it's like putting your hand out to stop a fall. Only here the paddle becomes your hand. When you feel yourself going over, you reach to that side and slap the back of the blade down flat on the surface. The momentary resistance of the impact will give you enough support to push yourself back up.

Notice that it is the back, or nonpower face, of the blade that is doing the work. To get it into position you may have to provide some wrist motion. When using a nonfeathered paddle, you will have to twist both wrists forward and straighten your arms to bring a blade into position for either a right- or left-side brace. When using a feathered paddle, the blade on the non-control-hand side is already in position for bracing. A brace on the control-hand side requires the wrist to be twisted forward and the arm straightened to position the blade. Here again is another example of the importance of keeping a set grip on the shaft.

Because you are pushing down for support, the structure of your body requires that the paddle be just to your side, or slightly behind your hips, to be effective. The brace will work best when you are in the last half of a forward stroke or sitting with the paddle horizontal and waiting to respond to a possible capsize.

In either situation, holding the paddle shaft as low and horizontal as possible is very important. When bracing, bring the paddle to horizontal and shift it laterally to the bracing side. Do not change your grip. You shift and, if need be, twist your wrists at the same time. Both arms will have elbows bent and raised, and the hand of the nonbracing arm will be held close to your stomach. Remain flexible at the waist and keep your upper body vertical.

Using this extended lever, slap with the back of the blade. You only need to spank the water firmly, not beat it into submission. If it sounds like a .357 magnum has gone off, you've overdone it. Keep the other blade low, so the shaft stays level and the bracing blade hits as flat and with as much surface area as possible. Once it hits, push down to bring yourself and the boat back up.

Because the slap only gives momentary support, you must regain your balance and recover the blade immediately. If you're fast, you can just pull the blade back to its starting position. But if you wait an instant too long, it begins to sink, losing its ability to bear your weight as it goes down. If you try to pull the blade up while it is submerged, you will encounter the same resistance that braced you when you slapped down, resulting in a capsize because you will pull yourself over. The only way to extract the blade is to rotate it to vertical by twisting your wrist back, then slicing the blade up and out as you push forward. The action is to roll the blade up, forward, and out. Recovery should be smooth, fast, and precise, without letting the blade sink too deep.

For the slap brace to be effective, it must become a reflex. Practice every chance you get: on both sides, eyes closed, or with the help of others standing next to the kayak trying to throw you off balance.

| 1 | 2 | 3 |
| shift over | slap! | rotate and pull up |

LOW BRACE

There's nothing inferior about the low brace. The "low" in low brace refers only to the position of the hands, not its effectiveness. The term is also a designation for a family of strokes with similar traits. All low braces require you to push palms-down on the shaft, as if doing a push up, to get support. They also use the back, or nonpower face, of the blade, and are held out to the side or rear quadrant of the boat. In addition to the standard low brace, there are two others: the slap, for quick recovery; and the sweeping, for longer support.

The low brace is directly related to the slap brace in that your hand and arm positions are all basically the same. The only difference is that the low brace requires the boat to be moving so you can use the lift from a skimming blade for support. If you are thrown off balance while paddling forward, a low brace will give you plenty of assistance and time to recover. The paddle is held to the side with the bracing blade's leading edge tilted up. The blade's climbing angle produces lift that you can then lean on.

Blade angle is very important. Too steep an angle produces a lot of drag, which will slow the boat and not provide enough support. A very shallow angle gives lots of support with very little drag, but its leading edge can be easily tripped and suddenly changed to a diving angle. If this happens, immediately release your grip and let the blade go its own way, otherwise it will take you with it. In the beginning it is better to err on the side of caution, so use a good, steep climbing angle and work down from there.

To brace, hold the paddle shaft low and horizontal, extend it over the bracing side, and bring it down. When you feel the first signs of lift, put your weight over the blade and push yourself up. The action is down and forward. To increase leverage, you can pull up with the nonbracing arm while you push down with the bracing one. The result of all this is a very stable position as long as the boat keeps moving and the blade stays on the surface.

Eventually the kayak will slow to a point at which the lift will no longer be adequate. Before this occurs, you should be up and retrieving the blade with an upward twisting of the wrist and a raising of the arms. As seen from the side, the blade skims forward, up, and out. If you don't make it up in time, the low brace can be linked into a sculling brace (see page 76) for continuous support as the boat stops.

Another linking possibility is with the stern rudder stroke. By bringing the paddle a little more forward than is usual for a stern rudder and using the back of the blade with a climbing angle, you can perform what is known as a low brace turn. This imparts a wide arcing curve and gives enough support in the rear quadrant for you to lean the boat over to tighten the turn.

The skimming action of a low brace can also be used while you are being pushed sideways by a broadside wave or surf. To stabilize yourself, extend your paddle so it skims on top and a little behind the wave as you are driven sideways. It's a good way to keep from rolling over.

SWEEPING LOW BRACE

There are times when you'll have to add some sweeping motion to a low brace to make up for its one major drawback: It is absolutely useless if the boat isn't moving through the water. Unlike the low brace, which needs forward movement in order to be effective, the more dynamic sweeping low brace makes its own. Whenever you feel like you're losing it, with the kayak dead in the water or barely gliding to a stop, go to a sweep. Or use it to lean on when you need to take time out for a look around or to catch your breath.

Another good reason to add in some sweep is to increase the power of the brace. Like the reverse sweep stroke, the sweeping low brace uses the unwinding of the larger muscles of the torso. Anatomically this motion is very forceful and easy to execute. It's a power that comes from the upper body being directly centered over the paddle so you can really put your weight into it. This in turn enhances the stability of the stroke and your ability to recover. The stroke also swings the blade over a broad area, giving you a wide range of support. As you can see, the sweeping low brace is a very potent recovery tool and belongs in the front line of your defenses.

The sweep starts with the paddle shaft held low and close to horizontal. The bracing arm is practically straight with some bend to act as a shock absorber; the hand of the other arm is in close to the stomach. With the paddle extended like this, the hand of the nonbracing arm acts like a pivot, with almost all power coming from the twisting of the body and some from the pushing of the bracing arm. Do not try to pull back with the inside hand as on a reverse sweep. Bring the back of the blade down as far to the rear as you can and swing it for-

ward in a low, broad arc. Hold the shaft loosely and start the push with the heel of the palm. At the completion of the stroke, when the paddle is perpendicular to the boat or about even with your hips, withdraw the blade sharply with a firm push down and forward. If you are not already there, this last shove should bring you all the way back up.

As in other braces, blade angle will affect performance. The steeper the angle, the closer the stroke comes to being a reverse sweep and providing more turning force than lift. A flatter angle will give you more lift than directional control. There are nuances here that, for the sake of maximizing efficiency, should not be ignored.

Low braces, and in particular the sweeping low brace, are the most dependable and easiest to use of all the support or recovery strokes. They link in with almost every other stroke and make a good, general safety net that even experts fall back on when they find themselves over their heads.

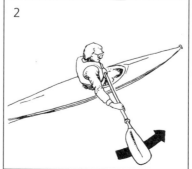

HIGH BRACE

Our bodies require a different type of stroke for bracing with the paddle in the forward quadrant of the boat. From your hips forward, it is both awkward and ineffectual to try to push yourself up by the back of a blade, as you do with low braces. Your only option is to brace with the blade's power face. Recovery is made by pulling down on the shaft and hanging from it, as if doing a chin-up, with your palms facing up and elbows pointing down. While the low brace lets you get right over the paddle and push down with all your weight, the high brace offers less leverage but greater potential for recovery at extreme angles.

There is a danger, and a bit of an inconsistency, in thinking that a high brace should be held high. Actually, high braces should be performed quite low to the kayak. To do otherwise risks shoulder strain or even dislocation. So keep your high braces low, the paddle shaft as level as possible, elbows close to the body, and hands never going above your head.

For bracing on either side with a nonfeathered paddle, or the control-hand side of a feathered paddle, blade angles are changed by twisting the wrist or wrists back and, if needed, bringing the forearms up. When bracing on the non-control-hand side of a feathered paddle, you will have to rotate the blade through 180 degrees. This requires the moderate contortion of bringing your elbow forward, forearm up, hand to your shoulder, and twisting the wrist all the way back. It is a weak position but, if held near the body, will be safe.

The high brace is used with two kinds of blade motions, either a downward pull or a skimming sweep.

The downward pull is used when you are thrown off balance while paddling forward with the paddle anywhere forward of your hips. To catch yourself, reach out about 3 feet and slap the surface with the flat of the power face. Pull the blade down and toward you with the bracing arm, while using the other arm as a pivot held close to your body. As the blade goes deeper and the shaft angle steepens, there will be a corresponding reduction in support. If you're fast, or recover balance quickly, you will be able to pull the paddle in toward you and back to its starting position. If you're not fast, which is more likely, you will have to retrieve the blade by rotating it 90 degrees aft and slicing it up and out.

Another downward-pulling motion is used when you are thrown off balance by a broadside wave or surf that is too high for a low brace. Extend your paddle into the upper portion of the wave with a high brace, and as you are driven sideways, support comes from hanging on the shaft and pulling the blade downward in the wave.

A skimming sweep motion is used for the sweeping high brace, which can also be incorporated into the forward paddling stroke. It is a simple matter to convert the forward stroke into a brace by angling the blade back from vertical. Because there is no need to lift the blade, reaction time and your chance for recovery are excellent. With the proper climbing angle you'll get plenty of support over a broad arc, giving a usable range from all the way forward to just ahead of your hips. To the rear of this the brace weakens considerably until, just behind your hips, it is no longer viable. End the sweep by pulling your upper arm down and the lower arm back. This will slice the blade up and out aft. Or you can link it with almost all of the propulsion, maneuvering, and even some of the low brace strokes.

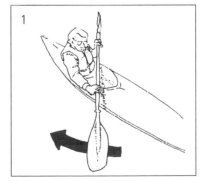

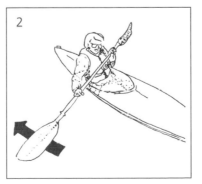

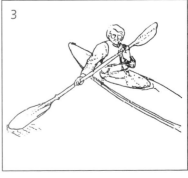

SCULLING BRACE

Think of the sculling brace as a never-ending sweeping brace. By moving the blade forward and back with its leading edge angled up each time it changes direction, you turn the paddle shaft into an unfaltering handle of support. With this you can maintain a firm stance or pull yourself up from some very extreme angles, regardless of what is going on around you. Where slapping gives you a brief moment and sweeping a few seconds, sculling can provide support for as long as you keep the paddle in motion.

Not all unbalancing forces are short jabs; some, like the winds preceding a squall or waves caused by a tidal rip, can feel like a hand pressing down on you. To get through these you will have to take a prolonged defensive posture by leaning into them and sculling on the windward side. During a rescue or any other circumstance demanding stability for protracted periods, you should opt for the sculling brace. There will also be times when you are knocked so far over that slapping or sweeping is impossible. In these situations your only way out may be to scull yourself back up with this versatile and powerful brace.

A sculling brace need not always be a high brace. It can also be done by holding the paddle as if for a low brace. Although this is a strong stroke, it cannot be used once the kayak has leaned past a rather shallow angle. It is therefore recommended that, for ultimate security at all angles, you learn and rely primarily on the high sculling brace.

The sculling motion must be constant, with every movement contributing to promoting lift, even during the switching of directions. The paddle is held out perpendicular to the boat and as close to horizontal as you can, providing the largest possible surface for lift. All power and sweeping motion comes from the hand and forearm on the bracing side, with the other hand held close to the body as a pivot for the shaft. Confine the stroke to a 45-degree arc (about a 3-foot sweep) directly to the side, going near neither bow nor stern.

The blade is kept on or near the surface, power face down, sweeping either forward or aft with the leading edge angled upward.

Blade-angle switching is done as in feathering with a quick twist of the control-hand's wrist. The control hand (or hands, when using a nonfeathered paddle) always directs the angle. This is true whether the control hand is in the upper or lower position. The cycle should be smooth and feel continuous, with no stopping where blade angles switch. Seen from the side, the paddle travels in an elongated, very shallow and flat figure eight. The blade may climb slightly upward during the stroke. Remember not to pull down sharply at the end of either the fore or aft stroke; rather, make a quick but fluid transition to the opposite direction, concentrating on smooth wrist motion. This keeps the pull steady and the motion uninterrupted.

Once perfected (this may take more strength and practice than other strokes), you will be able to hang from the paddle and lean way over; the farther over you go, the more compressed the stroke. The stroke will become flatter, shorter, and faster. It will take time to get to this point, but one of the nice things about practicing the sculling brace is that you have plenty of time to analyze what you are doing.

HEADING OUT

If you've gotten this far, you're hooked! And it's a fortunate thing, too, because what follows is the heart of sea kayaking: the good stuff. With the lessons in SK 102 you will solidify your education as a sea kayaker. You'll learn to make informed choices about additional equipment and evaluate the opinions of experts on a variety of topics. And you'll end up ready to head out to explore the world in your own boat.

Although SK 102 is not structured as such, it can be thought of as an introduction to the principles of circles of defense. These circles are nothing more than intentionally redundant safety measures. If one defense fails, another is there to take its place. The most important circle of defense is your skill: this is the best place to center your energies and hopes. Soon you will begin to understand how much more seaworthy you and your kayak can be. It's about control. You'll no longer be reacting to what the boat does to you. From now on, it will be the boat reacting to what you do to it. This is true mastery of your vessel, and it's a little scary because your limits become very obvious. A good seaman understands these limitations and works with them. A poor seaman is clouded in vanity and has an unrealistic vision of his or her capabilities. Stay objective, practice and paddle with others, and respect what you don't know. The Eskimo roll is one of the best components of your circles of defense. It is challenging to learn; many paddlers never do and, yes, they do just fine without it. But this is probably a mistake because no other recovery skill is as fast or complete as an Eskimo roll. Another important circle of defense—probably the most important—is your understanding of the waters you paddle on. In the pages that follow you'll explore your environment and learn the basics of good seamanship.

It is a timeless tradition of the sea not to put your faith in any one skill or piece of equipment. This is the philosophy of the realist. Know your ship, the waters you sail on, and yourself, and be prepared for anything.

Some equipment can make paddling easier and safer. It is a good outer circle of defense. Get the best you can afford. When choosing what you will need, think about what might go wrong and then get things to help with those situations.

There is something very satisfying about equipment. It is almost as if you were buying security. Most of it looks so dependable and reassuring, and when used wisely it can be. But very often the passion for equipment is the hiding place of those hoping to purchase what can only be achieved through skill. Choose products with discretion, use them wisely, but don't depend solely on your equipment to save you in an emergency.

Remember that sea kayaking is an education that never ends and always fascinates. Bon voyage!

WHAT YOU WILL NEED

9

SAFETY GEAR

Clothing

Beginners often see dressing for kayaking as a problem because it involves three separate environments: the air, the water, and the inside of the kayak sealed by the spray skirt. These three environments seem to have incompatible comfort and protection requirements. The air could be warm, the water cold, and the atmosphere inside the kayak like a steam bath.

When conditions are moderate and your bracing and rolling skills are in top form, you can eliminate at least one of these variables. If there is no need to dress for extended immersions and the water is warm, your only worries will be the outside air and the inside of the kayak, not the water: that is, not the water directly below you. You'll still be getting wet from spray and an occasional wave, but this can be taken care of by a lightweight paddling jacket. If the air is warm, you may not even want that, doing just fine in a bathing suit and T-shirt. For times when you're just not sure, opt for safety and dress for a possible dunking in water that can conduct heat away from your body about 25 times faster than air.

As the air cools or wind increases (wind chill), clothing for your upper body becomes more important. The best way to approach dressing for sea kayaking is with a system in which you layer clothes.

The layer closest to your skin needs to be breathable, allowing perspiration to evaporate. Cotton is one of the worst fabrics for this job. It readily absorbs moisture, is a poor insulator when wet, and dries slowly so you stay cold longer. The best baselayer fabrics are open weaves of impermeable fibers such as polyester. Chemically treated, they dry quickly and do not absorb perspiration.

The intermediate layer should create a thermal barrier, an air trap for insulation. The wide range of weights available, from thin, stretchy fleece to heavier, looped synthetic pile, allows you to choose the weight most appropriate for your paddling temperatures. Wool is a last resort; it becomes heavy and cumbersome when wet.

The outer layer should keep air in for improved insulation, but it should also keep you and your clothing dry. Moisture comes from within in the form of perspiration, so there has to be good ventilation, which can be mechanical (underarm or front-pocket flaps that open) or automatic (fibers or laminates that are both waterproof and breathable). Moisture also comes from without, in the form of spray and waves, so there has to be adequate waterproofing and good seals at the wrists and neck.

For all layers, just make sure the garments don't bind in the shoulders, arms, or torso.

You have to take care of your extremities, too. Your head, hands, and feet all require protection at one time or another. Head gear in warm weather can be anything that will keep the sun off, won't blow away, and can be soaked in water to be worn wet for keeping cool. In colder weather more than half of your body heat is lost through your head. So by taking your hat on and off you have a manually adjustable thermostat. Probably the best hat is a wool watch cap. Hoods on paddling jackets or windbreakers are good for wind and rain protection and work well if they do not restrict head motion. As an alternative to a hood, some folks use the traditional Sou'wester rain hat. They are less restrictive of motion, but tend to make the wearer look like a character on the box of frozen fish sticks. In very foul and cold weather when a capsize is a

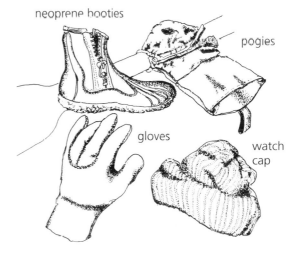

neoprene booties

pogies

gloves

watch cap

81

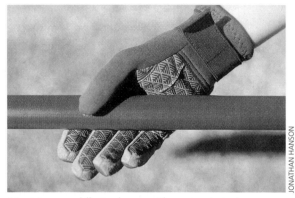

JONATHAN HANSON

Neoprene paddler's gloves with sure-grip palms are perfect for cold-water paddling.

distinct possibility, a neoprene hood is best.

Hands do best when they are kept dry and warm. Your first defense is good and well-placed drip rings on the paddle shaft. For cold water or foul weather, neoprene paddling gloves made for kayakers with grippy material on the palms and fingers are best. In really cold weather, gloved hands can be sealed in gadgets called pogies. These are gauntleted mittens that fit around the paddle shaft. You slip your hands in and grip the shaft directly. Practice all your rescue maneuvers while wearing your gloves to be sure they don't hinder you. If they do, buy different gloves.

Even though they are safely tucked away down in the sealed cockpit, your feet also need some protection. Their biggest hardship is getting the kayak to and from the water. Again, the choice of footwear is wide. Paddlers have used sandals, socks, old sneakers (keep laces short so they don't get caught on anything), and rubber boots. Neoprene booties made especially for sea kayakers are a good choice. These booties have rigid soles and good support for walking. A common problem with most footwear for kayaking is abrasion on your heels from the inside of the hull. Very few pieces of foot gear are protected in this area, so you might have to pad the hull where your heels touch. This gives the added benefit of improved boat control through another solid contact point and, if the weather is warm, the ability to get by barefooted.

Paddling Jacket

Paddling jackets have been designed to act as the final outer skin in your layering system. They are reminiscent of the original Eskimo anorak, which covered the paddler from hooded head down to where the garment bellied out so it could be very securely fastened around the cockpit coaming. It was as watertight as possible, and pretty much kept the wearer trapped in the kayak no matter what.

Today's paddling jacket is a little more forgiving and versatile than the traditional anorak. It is also not intended to be absolutely watertight. If you capsize, some water will find its way in as you roll back up. This is acceptable because its purpose is to shed waves and spray, provide a dead air space for insulation, and also (unlike the anorak) provide some ventilation. Excess heat and body moisture were no problems to the Eskimos, but for those of us kayaking in more hospitable waters it can be a nuisance. So a good paddling jacket should have ways to let you vent off this built-up steam. The material should be lightweight, waterproof nylon or something similar. Today's waterproof-breathable fabrics are an excellent choice.

The fit should be loose around the shoulders and upper arms to allow unrestricted motion, and roomy around the body to leave room for undergarments. You'll want the wrist openings to be as waterproof as possible to keep annoying paddle drips from rolling down your arms. Lightweight neoprene is the most commonly used material for jackets, with adjustable Velcro tabs to keep the seal tight. Elastic knitted materials won't work because they absorb water and stretch out of shape. Neck closures are a bit tricky in that a really good seal can almost strangle you.

paddling jacket

Absolute watertight integrity is not important because you want to be able to release built-up body heat and moisture. Look for a high, mandarin collar design, and maybe a hood that can be rolled up and secured out of the way when not in use. Because the garment is not going to be absolutely waterproof, it is safest if the waist is not sealed. A completely closed jacket could hold enough water to drag you down. Drawstrings, toggles, or elastics are adequate.

Nice extras are a Velcro-sealable pouch in front, a pocket on the sleeve, and sealable vents under the arms or on the chest.

Wet Suit

When sea conditions deteriorate, water temperatures go below 65°F, or there is any chance of having to spend a prolonged time in the water (no matter what the temperature), your choice of what to wear becomes a lot more serious.

One of the most popular ways of protecting yourself from loss of body heat is with some form of wet suit, either neoprene or thermal-stretch. Thermal-stretch, a synthetic fleece laminated to a waterproof-breathable fabric, is lighter than neoprene and thus offers less protection in cold conditions, but it is more comfortable and is an excellent choice for a broad range of paddling conditions. Neoprene is rubber that is expanded with millions of tiny air bubbles, making it both a good insulator and a source of flotation. One of its drawbacks is that neoprene retains moisture and becomes uncomfortably clammy after you have worn it a while. This situation can be improved by wearing clothing made of a stretchy polyester under the wet suit.

Fit is obviously an important factor for any wet suit. It must be snug enough to insulate well, but not so tight that movement is difficult. Before buying, try sitting to make sure you can still breathe and aren't being confined in the seat or crotch. Suits come in thicknesses of 3 mm for warm water paddling, 5 mm for general purpose use, and 6 mm for colder waters. The last choice is quite thick and may interfere with body rotation. Check first before buying. Your choices in wet suit styles follow.

Full wet suit. For cold water conditions, a full wet suit designed specifically for sea kayakers is the top choice for overall protection. Make sure the fit allows for full arm rotation.

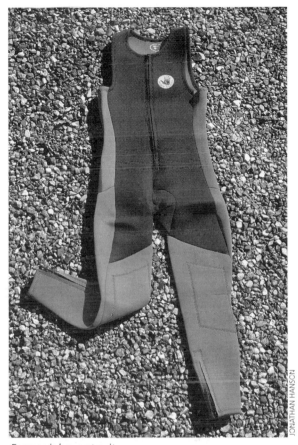

Farmer john wet suit.

Farmer johns. These are like a full wet suit with its arms cut off at the shoulder, leaving a bib in front and a high back. This gives you a combination of good protection for moderate conditions and freedom of movement. Because they cover so much of the body, 5-mm farmer johns and a paddling jacket might be sufficient for year-round kayaking in moderate climates.

Shorty. Same as a farmer john but with the legs cut off just above the knees. A shorty keeps the body's core protected and can be used to extend the season on each side of summer.

Vest. Covers only the absolute minimum and is good for light summer duty, or under a dry suit. Some vests are fitted with nylon sleeves to create a practical variation on the paddling jacket theme.

Wet suits only work when you wear them. If the conditions are serious enough to warrant the use of one, put it on before going out. Trying to climb into the suit after a dunking is the height of folly. It's almost impossible to do, and the impact of the cold water will have already taken its toll.

Dry Suit

If you're trying to stay warm in cold water, it is better to be dry than wet. Ideally, a dry suit lets you dress in the right clothing for the day by layering garments and then covering them with a watertight suit made of coated rubber or Gore-Tex. Unlike a wet suit, a dry suit has no insulating properties. It depends solely on the clothing it is protecting and the enclosed dead-air space to keep you warm. And it *will* keep you warm, much warmer than a wet suit. Dry suits are a serious step toward cold-water protection. The fact that you are even considering a dry suit indicates that you plan to encounter some very dangerous sea conditions and water temperatures that might be substantially below 50°F. Also, give some thought to not wearing a dry suit. With moderate water temperatures and minimal risks of immersion, a dry suit can cook you like a pork chop in a Shake 'n Bake bag. Overdressing, especially in a dark colored suit on a sunny day, can result in heat exhaustion.

There is no doubt that keeping water away is your best cold-weather defense. But all defenses have their price; dry suits are more expensive than wet suits. For this money you do get a lot more cold water protection and comfort. If the right clothes are used, and it is best to dress a little light because you will be generating your own heat, a dry suit can provide the perfect environment.

Dry is also a very relative term when applied to rubber dry suits. Because of the dampness generated by body heat and moisture that has no where to go, it is very difficult to both vent a rubber dry suit and keep it perfectly watertight. That's where a Gore-Tex suit, which is a lot more expensive, works very well; some body moisture vents through the fabric, but the fabric will still keep you dry.

The weakest points of any dry suit are the seals at the wrists, ankles, and neck. They are intended to stop the circulation of air and water without cutting off the circulation of blood. Entry zippers on one-piece suits also bring their share of potential problems and leaks. Rear-entry suits seem to leak less than the front-entry type, but you will require help

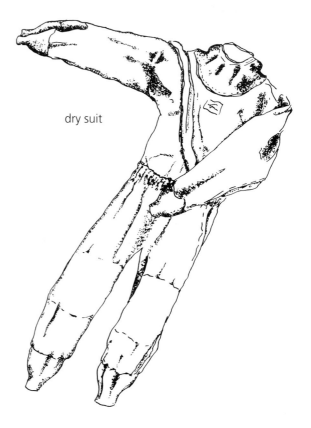

dry suit

putting one on. Surprisingly, some of the most waterproof suits are the two-piece variety because the seam between the jacket and pants can be sealed so well. Some of these suits also give you the important option of using the jacket on its own.

A dry suit's fit should be roomy enough to cover a full range of clothing, but not so bulky as to get in the way when paddling. Too much air held in the suit can be awkward or even dangerous when swimming. Consider what might happen with a lot of air trapped in the legs. This is why dry suits have to be "burped" to expel all excess air.

Luckily, because of the growing popularity of boardsailing and sea kayaking, there are plenty of dry suits available. But avoid the heavier suits that are used for diving. They are too restrictive and unnecessarily expensive. Whichever type you choose, think long and hard before buying. You may not even really need one.

Visual Distress Signals

Nobody likes to talk about dire emergencies in sea kayaking, but they can happen. There may come a time in your paddling career when you are overwhelmed by circumstances. It can happen to anyone through a lapse of judgment or a surprise occurrence. It is best to acknowledge this possibility and prepare for it. By doing this you will keep yourself realistically outfitted and in compliance with the law.

The U.S. Coast Guard requires kayaks to carry visual distress signals only at night (between sunset and dawn). This rule includes all inland waters and the Great Lakes, too.

You have three options: an electric distress light, which is a high-intensity flashlight that automatically sends the SOS code four to six times per minute; a strobe light; or flares. Each has its advantages and disadvantages for kayaking. Electric lights and strobes do not command immediate attention, have limited range when low in the water, and are adversely affected by conditions of poor visibility. The last option, flares, is the best. Flares have none of the disadvantages of the first two, and they are useful during the day. To meet regulations there must be at least three handheld or aerial flares aboard labeled as being coast guard approved, with an expiration date that does not exceed 42 months from the date of manufacture (not purchase), and stowed to be "readily available."

When a situation occurs that warrants the use of flares, keep in mind the two stages of a rescue: to alarm and to direct. Alarm devices must get people to stop, turn around, and look, which can be a surprisingly difficult job even in urban areas. To do this, use aerial flares, which overcome your limited line of sight and make a loud noise at the same time. Once you've gotten their attention, you have to keep rescuers aware of your position so they can be directed to you. To do this, use handheld flares or smoke generators.

Aerial flares are mostly for alarming. The idea is to get something bright as high up as possible for as long as possible and to make some noise while doing it. There are a wide variety available that are made mostly for yachting, such as self-contained launcher/flares. More versatile but clumsier to deal with and requiring the use of two hands are the 25 mm flare pistols, which can send up all sorts of rocketry. There are meteors, which are brief flaming balls

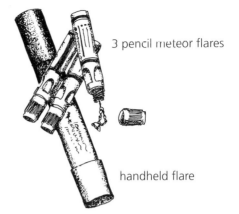

3 pencil meteor flares

handheld flare

that go high up and then directly down; or parachutes, which make a loud bang when they reach maximum altitude and then descend slowly. If you are going to bother carrying this sort of equipment, do not go half-way with only a 12-gauge gun; the devices it shoots are not worth the trouble.

A popular alternative to guns are small pencil meteor flares. They are sold in packages of three (so they fulfill the minimum coast guard requirements). These flares can fit in your pocket, are relatively inexpensive, and each has its own built-in launcher. They are a compromise among duration, brightness, and convenience. To compensate, carry a lot of them. When shooting any aerial flare, hold the launcher above your head and point it into the wind at a 60-degree angle to the horizon.

Directing rescuers to your position is best done with either handheld flares or smoke-generating devices. Unlike aerial flares, the handheld type last for longer periods and are less affected by winds. However, because they will be low to the water in a kayak, they offer a limited range of signal visibility. These flares work equally well in day or night conditions, whereas smoke-generating devices are only for daylight use. The U.S. Coast Guard approves only those generators, handheld or floating canisters, that put out smoke (usually orange) for at least 50 seconds. Smoke may be the best overall device for alarming and directing rescuers in bright sunlight on a windless day. Given a chance, the smoke cloud will rise to impressive heights and linger for some time over you. In less favorable conditions the smoke cloud may be held close to the surface or rapidly dispersed by strong winds. Potential rescuers may also find it impossible to see the smoke when looking into the sun or wind.

A good distress package consists of two parachute flares to alarm, three to six pencil meteor flares to alarm at close distances and for directing, one handheld flare for directing day or night, and a smoke generator for directing during the day.

All flares and signaling devices, even if they are designated "marine," are susceptible to the ravages of moisture and salt. They must be carefully stowed and protected to remain viable. But they also must be available when needed, the instant they are needed; you should not need to remove your spray skirt, dig into sacks, or anything else. The best arrangement is to carry some alarm signals on your person at all times. Use the pockets on your PFD or jacket, or clip a small one to the PFD. Keep the rest of the alarm signals on deck in a watertight container such as a resealable plastic bag and store the directing signals inside the boat if there is no room on deck.

Flares can cause as much trouble as they are meant to resolve. Many handheld flares drip molten slag as they burn, which can burn your skin or melt the kayak's deck. Hold the flares high on the downwind side and at an angle over the water. Even worse are the flares that do nothing. A high percentage of flares are duds, and you never know which ones they are until you try to light them (which is a good reason to carry more than you think you'll need). If a flare should fail to go off immediately, hold onto it for a few extra seconds. If it still does not ignite, throw it in the water and forget about it. Keep flares locked away from kids. Kids love them and are fully capable of sending up a warning rocket in your living room (which will get more results and attract more attention than any flare you'll ever launch on the water).

Lights

If you're traveling at night, it makes sense to carry a flashlight. It is also the law. The coast guard does exempt you from having to install electric red and green navigation lights on your kayak. Your only obligation as a paddler is to have at hand "a white light which shall be exhibited in sufficient time to prevent collision." Although not specified, the range of this light should be 2 miles. Keep the light secured in some way on deck so it is ready at a moment's notice. Obviously, waterproofing (not just water-resistance) and high intensity are desirable features.

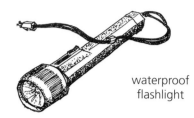

waterproof
flashlight

Radios and Cell Phones

Handheld VHF marine radios are your best method of communication on the water. Channel 16 is always monitored by the U.S. and Canadian coast guards and should be used in case of an emergency. There are dedicated channels for local weather reports and access to marine telephone operators to link you to a land phone line. The only limitation of handheld VHF marine radios is that the range is only up to 5 miles at best. And, because they are battery powered, they can only be used for a limited time until their power source must be recharged or replaced. For kayaking, only use VHF radios that are waterproof, and even better, ones that float as well.

Cellular phones do not fare well in a marine environment. But if protected from abuse and getting wet, they offer excellent backup to a VHF radio because almost all areas of the continental United States are covered for this service.

For personal communications between kayaks or you and someone on the beach, family radio service (FRS) is the way to go. Like the walkie-talkies you played with as a kid, these small (8-ounce) two-way radios are made for short distances—not more than 2 miles. But unlike a kid's toy, they are tough and waterproof. They give you more privacy than a VHF radio and cost less to use (free) than a cell phone. Some even have a built-in AM/FM receiver.

cell
phone
and holder

CAMELBAK

KNEE LIFT

To achieve dynamic stability (see page 48), a kayaker uses body motion to keep the kayak upright. What we'll explore here draws on the same principles. But instead of you reacting to what the boat does, it will now be the boat that does the reacting. This section is about controlling the side-to-side tilt of the kayak with your knees, which opens the way for a new set of paddling skills.

There are two ways to tilt a kayak. The first is called *leaning*, which is done by holding your upper and lower body as one unit and leaning over. The result is that the boat, as well as your body, goes over at an angle. This type of tilting puts your center of gravity off to one side and is inherently unstable unless it is used to compensate for forces in a fast turn (like a bicyclist going around a corner), which occur in whitewater kayaking but rarely in sea kayaking. A more stable and controlled way to tilt a kayak is by *edging*. This is done by staying flexible at your waist to separate the actions of your upper body from those of your lower body. The tilting force comes from your lower body pushing up through the knees while the upper body stays perpendicular to the water. The knee lifts up one side of the boat and the boat tilts while your center of gravity stays over it. You can tilt a kayak to some very extreme angles this way without losing balance or control.

What good is all this knee lifting? It can be used to raise a side of the kayak to allow it to slide over the water when going sideways with a draw or sculling stroke. It can tilt the boat over to get its ends out of the water, reducing the boat's waterline length and making stationary or moving turns easier. It can be used to turn the kayak while underway and is useful in waves or surf. When incorporated into any of the bracing strokes, a knee lift can provide that extra punch you need to bring you back up or it can be used on its own for less drastic recoveries.

To knee-lift a boat onto its side, bring the knee up on the side you want to raise. This is a lifting motion that starts by flexing the foot and raising the hip on the side to be raised, while at the same time depressing the hip and buttock on the other side. You are literally lifting one side of the boat so it is hanging from your knee while you are balancing on your opposite buttock. As a test, try alternately lifting one knee and then the other to rock the kayak. The sensation is that your hips are moving up and down, but actually it is your knees that are controlling the motion.

As with earlier examples of dynamic stability, a flexible connection between your upper and lower body is the key. To maintain balance, your upper body must stay upright and over the boat's center of buoyancy. Lean the boat, not your body. Because knee lifting uses muscles not commonly used, exercises that strengthen and stretch your torso can help. For example, do a knee lift on one side and hold the boat on edge for as long as you can. Repeat this on the other side.

How you fit within the kayak is critical to the success of a knee lift. Your lower body, from the hips down, should be connected to the boat. When it moves, the boat must move. Movement comes primarily from your groin, back, and abdominal muscles, and is directed to the boat through your knees and to a lesser extent your thighs if there is a good thigh-bracing system. There will be times when even greater forces must be absorbed from the momentum of a knee being driven up hard to prevent a capsize. So, the boat's knee braces must be well padded and strong.

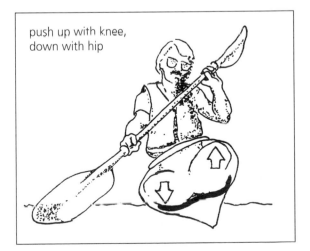

push up with knee, down with hip

CARVED TURNS

One of the most irritating experiences is trying to hold a course in a side wind when your boat wants to weathercock into it. You have to work constantly against the kayak's tendency to turn into the wind, which forces you to paddle harder or more frequently on one side, which in turn slows you down, ruins your paddling rhythm, and leaves you with sore muscles. In most cases a carved turn can eliminate or at least reduce this tiresome problem.

The carved turn works by edging the kayak enough to change its underwater shape to affect how it steers. If the boat is edged to the left, the pressures on the now asymmetrical shape of its waterline cause it to veer to the right. Try this with your own boat. Get going at a good clip and stop paddling when you feel you are going straight. If the boat is level, it should continue on course. Do this again, but when you stop paddling, knee-lift the boat to one side. More than likely the boat will slowly turn away from the side toward which the boat was tilted.

Most kayaks will respond in varying degrees. Some may have to be tilted way over before turning. Others are so seriously out of fore-and-aft trim or of such an extreme design that they will yaw off in an ever-tightening circle. Fortunately, these are rare cases.

In use, you will be paddling along and realize that you are putting more of an effort than you'd like into making the boat go straight. To compensate, tilt up the downwind side with a knee lift and continue paddling forward. If the wind is not too strong, your carved turn might be enough to counteract the boat's weathercocking. If it is not, you will have to paddle with a slight sweep stroke on the upwind side. This will be easier to do because the side you are sweeping on has been lowered and your upper body is still in an upright and efficient paddling position. Or, you can edge the boat over only when you make a stroke: upwind stroke, upwind edge; downwind stroke, no edge. If you want to increase your edging, add a bracing angle to the blade for extra support as you sweep. The same techniques can be used to keep the boat under control while paddling downwind, or to make small course corrections in calm water.

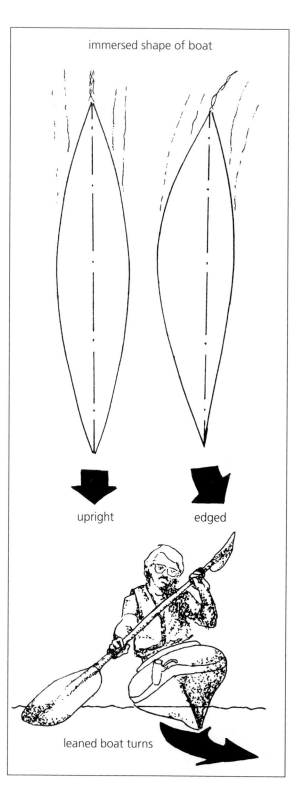

immersed shape of boat

upright   edged

leaned boat turns

HIP FLICK

There is a fine line between a knee lift and a hip flick, so fine that many kayakers do not even bother making the distinction. Terminology is, after all, relatively unimportant. What is important is visualizing that your knees do the lifting for the powerful muscles around your waist. If your upper body can be supported by something, such as a solid bracing stroke, then your lower body and the boat can be moved by the muscles in your torso. When these muscles are flexed (flicked), their momentum, coupled with the driving up of the knees, can force a boat over as well as bring it back up. Although it is the abdominal muscles doing the work, it feels like it's coming from your hips. This is why it's called a hip flick.

To learn the hip flick, you'll need a controlled environment and a friend standing by, just in case. Find a pool, a low dock, a ladder on a dock, or get your friend to stand in chest-deep water holding a paddle horizontal on the surface. What you're looking for is something solid to hold on to. Once you've learned the hip flick, you'll substitute a dependable bracing stroke for this solid training support.

Grab the support with both hands, palms facing down. Lean your body so your head, shoulders, and torso are in the water. Pull the kayak over onto its edge and hold it there just before the point of capsize. To bring the boat back up, hold your upper body in place and give a twisting flick at your waist, forcing your knee up against the low side of the boat. By connecting this flick to your lower body and then through your knees to the kayak, you should be able to impart enough of a sudden push to rotate the boat upright. It will feel as if the boat has been rolled back under you, and it has.

In the beginning there are two instincts that you must fight. The first instinct is using the strength of your arms to pull yourself up; rather, use the twisting of your torso muscles to rotate the boat. Ignore your arms as much as possible. They are there only to provide a point of balance. Your upper body should be completely isolated from the process, with all lifting and righting moments coming from the hip flick. You'll find that once you get the hang of it, you'll only need to hold the support with your finger tips; you'll feel no strain at all on your arms.

The second instinct that you must fight is to bring your head up first. Your head should be the last thing to leave the water as you roll up. Intuitively we want to get our heads up to breathe. But by doing so you work against righting the kayak. While in the water the head and torso are buoyed up, so they weigh less. Also, if the head and torso come up too soon, they raise your center of gravity, making it harder to right the boat. The idea is to flick the boat up with enough follow-through that it carries your body and head along with it. The order for rising should be the boat followed by your waist, torso, shoulders, and, last, your head.

Once you have the feel of recovering from a near capsize position with a hip flick, try a hip flick with the boat fully inverted. Holding on as before, capsize toward the support side. Once capsized you will experience tremendous stretching at your waist as you simultaneously hold your body near the surface and try to keep seated in the overturned kayak. Think of yourself as a taut spring being stretched to its limits. When ready, give your waist a sudden and sustained twist so this powerful spring can return to its coiled position, pushing your knee and the boat upward.

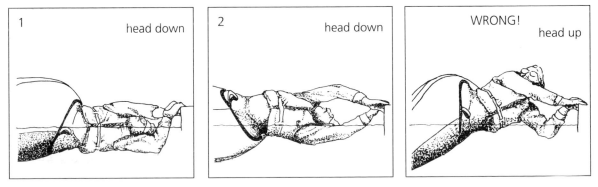

| 1 | head down | 2 | head down | WRONG! head up |

EXTENDED BRACING

The bracing stroke is a reaction to "Oops!," the feeling that you are going over. An extended bracing stroke is the reaction to "Oh my God!," the feeling that you are really going over and might not be coming back. As you push your abilities further, you'll find newer and more interesting ways of getting into trouble. Extended bracing will help you get out of them.

Extended bracing is a response to a critical situation. It's a holding action, giving you a solid support against which you can use a hip flick to get back up. It can also help maintain a defensive posture when you are overwhelmed and provide stability while performing unwieldy tasks or rescuing others. Obviously, it's good to learn how to extend oneself.

There are three ways of extending a brace. You can extend the paddle, extend your body, or combine the two.

Extending the paddle means altering your grip on the shaft. For general paddling it is not good policy to move your hands about. But things are not always that simple, and there will be times when you will want or need to maximize the paddle's leverage. Do this by shifting your hands upward along the shaft. Bring the upper hand to the throat of the upper blade and the lower hand to the middle of the shaft. To help your orientation, use the crook of the little finger of the upper hand to feel the edge of the blade. Maintain the same hand spacing as usual, and try to keep the shaft close in for the most effective use of your strength. An interesting variation of the extended paddle brace is to reverse it and substitute the crook of your shoulder for the center grip. This lets you scull the blade with one hand while you go about your chores with the other.

Extending your body requires immersing as much of your upper body and head as possible. This may sound counterintuitive, because the idea of bracing is to stay out of the water. But if you've gone over too far, you may have no choice. Or you may do it intentionally. For Greenland Eskimos in their ultra-narrow kayaks, this was standard procedure. By sculling and using the body's natural buoyancy, they could hold a very stable attitude for quite some time.

Trying to brace at extreme angles with your upper body hanging out over the paddle requires a lot of energy. You're asking the stroke to support almost your full weight. By lowering your head and upper body into the water, you reduce their weight through buoyancy and at the same time lower your center of gravity. This makes it easier to keep the kayak from going all the way over and gives you the time and security to bring yourself back up.

To get in position while bracing, twist at the waist so your back is to the water and you are leaning toward the rear of the boat. Face upward, keeping the back of your head in the water. It's like doing a back float while in the kayak. Once you've learned to relax in this nearly capsized position, you'll find that you can maintain it for quite some time. During all this the kayak will have a tendency to move about. Use your lower body and knees to keep it under control. When ready to come up, give a powerful hip flick and pull down on the paddle. Remember that the boat comes up first, followed by your torso, and, last, by your head.

You have to dedicate yourself fully to an extended brace in order for it to succeed. When you feel yourself going over don't give up. Try to brace, and brace hard. Be willing to fight and commit yourself to the brace. Extend the paddle, lower your head and body, and scull or pull up for all you're worth. For your first attempts you might want to practice in shallow water where you can push off the bottom if you can't hold the brace. It takes effort, finesse, timing, and balance to make an extended brace work, but in the end it will do the job.

Stabilizing yourself to perform a task.

Keeping yourself from going all the way over.

An eskimo roll will get you back upright. It's all technique, not strength.

ESKIMO ROLL

PRINCIPLES

There's nothing wrong with capsizing. It shows that you're exploring your limits, and that's good. The only problem is that each time you capsize, you've got to get out, get in, and start over again. Not exactly energy efficient, fun, or, in some conditions, safe. Plus, the thought of going through all that might make you afraid to take chances or experiment—and that's not good.

A way of recovering from a capsize without leaving the boat is the Eskimo roll, which is the fastest and most complete recovery skill available to the kayaker. The principle behind the roll is simple. After you have capsized, you sweep the paddle out as a bracing stroke from which you can pull and hip flick your way back up. Simple. At least it should be.

There seems to be some mystical image that goes with the Eskimo roll. Yet, contrary to popular belief, not all the aboriginal kayaking traditions included this ability. The Aleuts never used the roll, practicing a reentry method instead, and they got along fine for a few thousand years. It is not the end-all of rescue techniques. As long as you have one or two other ways of recovering, you'll probably get by.

But without it you will subconsciously develop a style that is interested more in staying upright than in efficiency. This makes you paddle defensively and plateau way below your natural level of ability. When you can roll, you become more self-sufficient and less anxious when things start to go wrong. Compared with other rescue methods, rolling is quick, works in rough water, reduces exposure, and requires a minimal outlay of energy. It's also fun. If you can, learn how to roll.

The Eskimo roll is not a superhuman feat, nor is it an advanced maneuver only for experts. It demands no more strength and skill than a strong brace. In essence, a roll is only a sweeping brace done upside down.

Once inverted, the paddler sets up for the roll with his or her body leaning forward and upward against the deck and the paddle on the surface ready to make a broad, sweeping brace stroke. As the sweep starts to bring the boat up, the paddler hip flicks to bring it the rest of the way. When the kayak is almost upright, the body and head are brought up with a forceful brace or draw at the end of the sweep.

The first recorded roll by a non-Eskimo was done in 1927 by the Austrian Hans Pawlata, who picked up the idea from the writings of Arctic explorers. Not only was he the first, but he was also one of the few persons who have ever learned to roll from a book. Learning to roll by yourself is neither easy nor safe, but with the information in this section, and some real dedication, you could learn to roll without anyone's help. However, it's unlikely.

If you can, get a knowledgeable instructor; someone to use as a role (roll) model who will coach you. At the very least have a friend standing by to help with the first few tries.

There are many types of rolls. The one described here is a modified screw roll, so called because the paddler looks like he or she is twisting through the water like a screw. It is one of the simplest and most reliable. There is no universal "best" roll, but the modified screw roll is close to it.

The roll can be explained by breaking it into its component parts. Learn the parts one at a time, while keeping in mind the place each has in the total process. When you can perform all the components, combine them into a full roll.

Before starting, you'll need to have the hip flick and extended high brace down pat. These two points are the foundation of all rolling. You'll also find a nose clip or face mask invaluable. Practice in warm water while wearing your PFD and spray skirt, and rest frequently to keep from getting dizzy. Almost anyone who puts his or her mind to it can roll. Even you.

PRACTICE: SETUP

The unnerving thing about a capsize is how suddenly it occurs. One moment you're breathing air, the next you're wishing you were one step back on the evolutionary ladder and had gills. I don't know if it's more of a shock when it's rough and you're expecting it, or when it's calm and it's the furthest thing from your mind. Either way, the first steps in having a foolproof roll start with being able to set up, whether you're in a maelstrom or on a pond.

If you have practiced regularly and with dedication, the setup position should be instinctual, but because very few of us are obsessively devoted to rolling, it should at least be mechanical. Get your setup to where it can be done by the numbers and you'll be alright. The best way is to develop a pattern and do it step-by-step each time, every time.

Before starting, you will have to choose which side to set up on. Most paddlers find that their "good" side is the one opposite their control hand. If your feathering is controlled by the right hand, set up on the left side. If you are paddling nonfeathered, determine the side on which your brace and hip flick is strongest and set up on the opposite side. If your strongest high brace is on the left, set up on the right. Once you've got that settled, sit in the kayak and go through the setup step-by-step.

The first step is twisting at the waist to get the paddle over the side and parallel to the boat.

The second step is to slide your rear hand to the base of the rear blade and your forward hand to the center of the shaft. Hold the base of the rear blade with your palm on its power face. You can usually tell the power face by tactile clues such as its curve or center ridge. If not, provide a clue with tape.

The third step is to set the angle of the forward blade, so its outer edge is angled upward to provide lift as it sweeps around. When practicing right side up, the outer edge will be angled downward. Your rear hand is the key to getting the correct blade angle. With feathered paddles, the rear hand, with the palm on the power face, is held with knuckles down and fingernails on the boat's side at the seam line. With nonfeathered paddles, use the same grip but keep your wrist cocked back so its underside touches the seam line. Check the forward blade to see that its power face is up (or down, when practicing right side up) and that it is at about a 30-

degree angle. Record this rear hand position in your mind.

The fourth step is to place the underside of the wrist of your forward hand on the seam line. This puts the shaft on a slight angle pointing up (or down, when practicing right side up) and out, away from the hull.

The fifth step is to lean forward as far as possible. If you can, bring your nose to the deck. In this tucked-in position, your head is protected and you are closer to the boat's axis of rotation, making it easier for you to right yourself.

That's it. Remember these five steps, practice them with your eyes closed, going strictly by feel, and you'll automatically get yourself into the setup position. To see if you've got it right, try setting up and capsizing. Have someone of reasonable strength stand next to you in waist-deep water. Get in the setup position and capsize. As you go over, keep your arms pressed tightly against the hull and exhale slowly through your nose, or wear a nose clip or face mask. When over, extend both hands as high as you can to get the paddle well clear of the water. To make sure that your forward blade is free, try to slap it on the surface. Have your helper check for blade angle and to see that the rear blade is held high enough to clear the boat's bottom during the sweep. When ready to come up, hit the boat three times. Your helper should reach over the bottom of the upturned kayak, grab its side, and pull you over. You can help by staying in a tucked position.

As a final test, capsize while in the normal paddling position and go to the setup after you've capsized. You'll find that the paddle winds up in the strangest places. Just stop, collect your thoughts for a second, and go through the steps one by one.

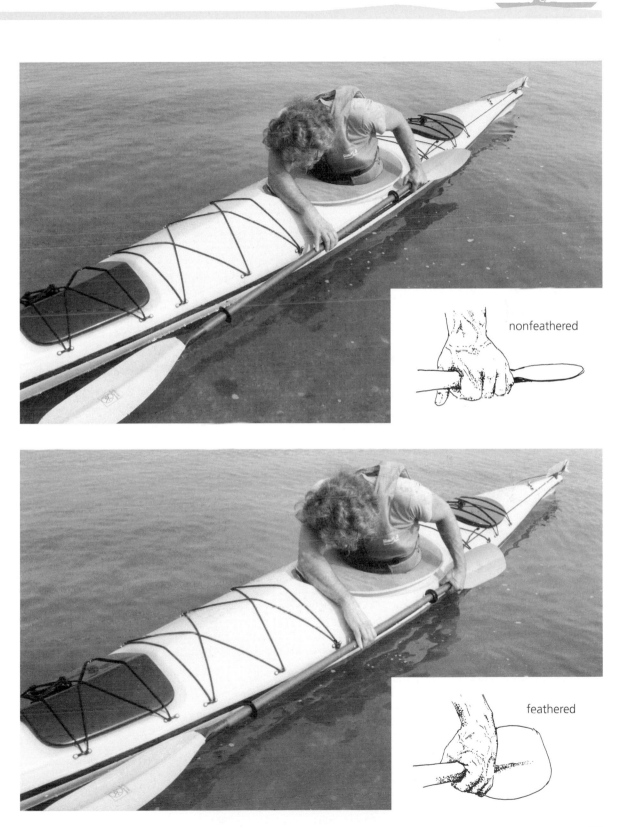

nonfeathered

feathered

PRACTICE: SWEEP

The blade's sweep across the water provides a supporting brace that gets you and the kayak most of the way up and the paddle into position for the hip flick. It is one of the trickiest maneuvers in kayaking, and definitely worthy of some extra help while practicing. The best place to get this help is from a solid-foam paddle float and an assistant.

When your float and assistant are all set, capsize with your helper standing off to the side you will sweep out on. When completely inverted, go through the steps of setting up, making sure to push both hands well above the water. Keep the rear arm bent and held high enough so the rear blade will clear the boat's bottom; check to see that the forward blade is in place by slapping it on the surface. To produce lift, the leading edge of the forward blade must be raised. Check that your rear wrist is in the proper position and cock your forward wrist to impart the proper angle.

Start the sweep with conviction and speed. The forward arm should be almost straight and swung around like a gate. The other arm should push up and forward to keep the inside blade from hitting the boat, forcing the sweeping blade down instead of out. Swing your whole body from the waist to use the full power of the muscles of your torso. It is nearly impossible to roll using only your arms. Think about sweeping out in a broad, level arc with the blade skimming along, or just below, the surface. It will support you and lift you.

During the sweep, your body, which was leaning forward in the setup, is now sweeping around with the paddle adding to its momentum. Your head and torso should follow the paddle's path. You may have to force the situation by holding your head against your arm, or keeping your eye on the blade (a diver's mask will help here). As you start your sweep, apply a strong knee lift on the side opposite the side on which you are sweeping out.

If all has gone well, as the paddle approaches the straight-out position, the kayak will have rotated halfway up and your body will be at the surface. When the paddle is perpendicular to the boat, stop the sweep; beyond this you lose power and can strain muscles. At this point you may need your assistant's help to get back up.

I know this is a lot to remember; in fact, you probably won't. Don't worry, in the beginning almost no one does. You'll make mistakes, such as sweeping off on the wrong side, but keep trying. Let your helper give you feedback by checking paddle and blade position or even directing the blade through the sweep for the first few times so you can get a feel for the motion.

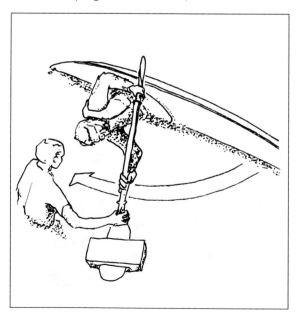

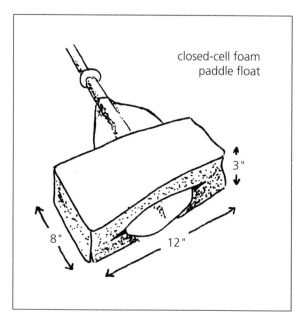

closed-cell foam paddle float

3"

8"

12"

The hip flick used in the Eskimo roll is pretty much the same as any other hip flick, the differences being when and how it's used and the addition of a sweeping lay-back motion.

Have your helper stand in waist-deep water on the side opposite your setup side. If you set up on your left when right side up, that becomes the boat's right when inverted, and the side you'll roll up on. So your helper should be on your right side (yes, it *is* confusing). Place your hands in their proper setup positions on the shaft. Put the paddle out perpendicular to the boat so your helper can hold the blade near the surface.

Using the paddle for support, lean the kayak over toward your helper and hip flick back up. Start at gentle angles, gradually progressing to going all the way over.

Because the hip flick and lay-back occur toward the end of the sweep, your head and body are coming up with the kayak and flowing back with the sweep all at the same time. It is important to continue the momentum of both. You will naturally come up as part of the hip flick; but now you must add that something extra that makes the rolling hip flick different from its generic cousin. You will have to lean backward as you are rolling up. The progression is this: the boat begins to come up, followed by your waist, which is starting to bend toward the rear deck, then your torso, which is swinging up and back, and finally your head, which is almost on the rear deck as the boat becomes level. Not only does this perpetuate the momentum of the sweep, it also lowers your center of gravity and brings the weight of your upper body closer to the kayak's axis of rotation.

You'll know you're getting it if, of course, you can right the kayak. But you'll know you're really getting it if your helper feels a reduction of pressure on the blade. The less pressure on the blade, the more effective your flick and lay-back. To further simulate the roll, have your helper hold the blade until you start. Your helper should then take his or her hands away so you can pull down hard against the water, using only its resistance for support. Once you've got that, it's just a matter of connecting the setup to your flick and lay-back with a sweep and you're rolling.

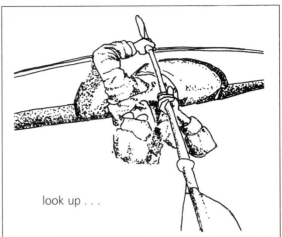

look up . . .

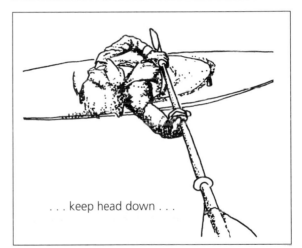

. . . keep head down . . .

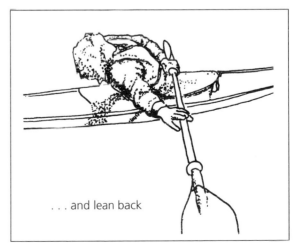

. . . and lean back

THE COMPLETE ROLL

In theory, joining the separate components of the setup, sweep, and flick and lay-back should enable you to perform an Eskimo roll. In practice, it is not quite that simple or straightforward; but it isn't too far off either.

Although the roll may be divided into separate practice components for the sake of learning, they must not be thought of as segregated movements. The roll should be one fluid motion. It starts with the outward sweep of the paddle and becomes an exaggerated dancer's motion with your body flowing out, around, back, and up. All components are integrated into one forceful drive to the surface.

You'll notice that the series of illustrations at right begins with the paddler already capsized. How you get there while practicing is your choice. For your first attempts you might want to setup while upright and stay that way while capsizing. Once you are able to roll from this prearranged setup, take it a step further by capsizing while in the paddling position. When you're OK with that, take it to the final stage by capsizing while actually paddling and underway.

After the confusion of an accidental capsize, when it finally sinks in that you're upside down, you must center your thoughts on getting set up. Even in the most tumultuous conditions you'll be able to accomplish a proper setup if you do it step by step. Paddle held over to the side. Hands in place on the shaft. Rear hand sets forward blade angle. Forward hand sets shaft angle. Lean forward. To make sure you're set, reach up with both hands to clear the surface, slap the water with the forward blade, and feel for the bottom of the boat with your back hand. See illustration 1 at right for setup.

From here it's technique plus determination that will roll you up. Although the overall motion must be flowing, it must flow with force. Once you start the sweep, keep going. Put your heart and muscle into it.

Power should come from the muscles of the torso, not your arms. Back this up with a rotating force from the lower hip and knee. The power face of the blade must be facing down and at about a 30-degree angle to ensure lift (illustration 2). If you are uncertain of the blade's angle, opt for a little more. Too much may slow down the sweep and reduce its effectiveness, but at least it won't dive and give you nothing at all.

As in the practice sessions, bring the sweep and your upper body out and around until they are perpendicular to the kayak's side (illustration 3). It is here that you trade the sweeping brace for the downward pull of the high brace. Let your body continue its motion of around, up, and back, while your arms begin to pull down and in. This is the moment of hip snap. Don't try to flick yourself up before this point—it will be futile. When the paddle is at 90 degrees to the boat, hip flick while laying back (illustrations 4 and 5). Timing is everything.

When it's time to flick up, do it with gusto. Bring your paddle down and past your head with a grand swinging motion. But remember that it's the boat you are flicking up, not yourself. Keep your head in the water until the last possible moment. First, get the boat up, followed by your waist, torso, shoulders, and, last, your head. Do it with an arching back to keep your body as low and close to the rear deck as possible (illustration 6). Stay flexible. Think of your waist as a giant universal joint connecting your hips and the boat to your upper body.

Once up, try to stay that way. Sometimes the momentum that rotated you up can keep you going right around and back over again. There is also a second or two of disorientation on being upright. In this condition you may need a moment to let your mind catch up to your body. To stabilize yourself, keep your paddle in the water and be prepared to make a few short sculling strokes for support (illustration 7).

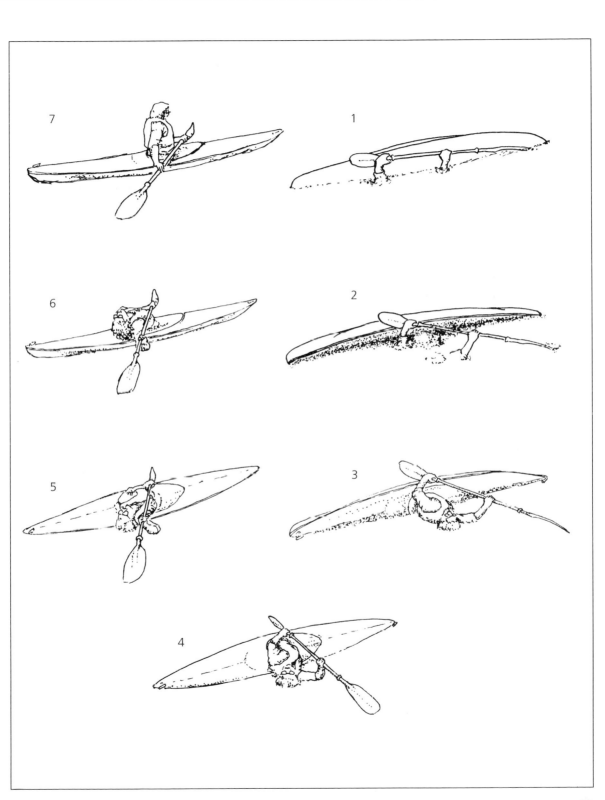

FINE POINTS

Learning to roll is an important art, there is no doubting that. But, no matter how proficient you get, don't rely on it as your sole means of recovery from a capsize. Rolling is not an infallible system. Learn and practice at least two alternative methods of self-rescue as security backups. Good choices are the paddle float reentry, and the reentry-and-roll. Also, work even harder at developing a reliable line of defense against capsizing, such as bracing. To paraphrase a well-known kayaking instructor: mastering the Eskimo roll is a measure of success; having to roll is a measure of defeat. Although this is an extreme view, there is some truth behind it. Looked at in a more positive way we could also say that knowing how to roll is good but knowing how not to need to roll is better.

Sometimes a capsize can't be avoided because of conditions, and you're forced to roll. When caught like this, your bracing skills may not be up to the job; there are limits. Most often we find ourselves beyond these limits because we've ignored the most primary defense system of all against capsizing—good judgment. If it was wind or waves as opposed to your own clumsiness that knocked you over, the rugged situation you left on the surface will be there waiting for you when you roll back up. Be ready to go into a defensive bracing posture when you come back to the surface so it doesn't happen again. There is the well-known anecdote of the kayaker who paddled and rolled (three strokes to every roll) across a particularly nasty patch of water. There's no reason for this to ever happen to you. Paddling is definitely more fun without having to roll.

The roll shown in this book is a modified screw roll, a compromise between two other rolls: the Pawlata (or extended paddle) and the standard screw roll. The paddle and body movements are similar for all three: you set up, sweep out, and hip flick back up. The main difference is in how the paddle is held.

In the Pawlata roll, named for Hans (or Edi to his friends) Pawlata, the hand grip is very extended. Back then, Edi's idea of rolling was to lever the body and boat up with no thought of using the hip flick. Naturally he wanted the longest lever possible to get the most power, so he grabbed the rear blade by its tip with one hand, placing his forward hand a little behind the center of the shaft. It was like swinging around a long pry bar. It would get you up with a minimum amount of finesse; but your grip on the paddle would be tenuous, making this style of roll

slower to perform and shaky in rough water. The Pawlata roll is still used today as a training exercise for beginners wishing to graduate to the screw roll.

The screw roll is a good proven general-purpose roll. The best thing about it is that your hands stay in their normal paddling positions. This means there is less confusion in setting up, and more security once you're back on top of the water. Because your leverage is less than that for the modified screw, and much less than that for the Pawlata, good technique is very important to ensure the success of the screw roll.

As you can see, the modified screw roll is somewhere in between these two. It's a good place to start. But if you're having trouble, try the Pawlata roll to at least get you going and give you the feeling that you might actually learn to roll someday. Work with either style, refine it, and then go on to the screw roll as your final goal.

As you become more involved in sea kayaking, and as you further explore what it has to offer, you will discover that there are a lot more Eskimo rolls than the three types described here. I know of ten offhand, and I'm sure there are more. Some are useful, and some are stunts or of historical interest only. Once you can perform something that at least looks like a roll, study these other types with the goal of defining your own style. Always keep in mind that if it works and works all the time and can be done quickly and safely, it's a good roll.

The advantage of learning the modified screw roll is that it emphasizes the importance of a solid hip flick and lay-back. This is good, because if there is one thing that could be pointed out as the most common problem area in rolling, it would be the hip flick. And within the hip flick, the biggest problems are not laying back and having your head come up too early.

The hip flick is important because if you're good at it, you can roll without a paddle. There are stories of Eskimos using broken paddles, harpoons, or knives to perform a roll; some contemporary paddlers can get by using only their hands. This means that whatever it is you are using to sweep out, while important, it is secondary to your timing. The sweep merely rotates you up to the point where your body can provide some positive buoyancy. From there on it is the released energy of the hip flick that does the rest.

But even this can be subverted if you succumb to the natural instinct of wanting to get your head out of the water and into the air as soon as possible.

Your brace can be strong, but it will be hard-pressed to overcome the offset center of gravity of a head and body lifted out of the water. Remember that the weight of your head and body is reduced in the water through their own buoyancy (plus that of your PFD); this gives your body motion a better chance to get the boat up so you can follow through.

If it is hard to envision or understand the reason for having the boat come up first and not you, think of a falling cat. Cats almost always land on their feet. They do this by righting themselves in mid-air. As they fall, they quickly bring their head around so it is level, and then follow through by bringing their body around to line up with their head. You should be doing essentially the same thing with your hip flick. First roll the boat up and then follow through by bringing your body around, allowing the motion of the boat and your hip snap to help pull you up.

Another common problem area in rolling is having the paddle dive as it sweeps around. This can be caused by one of three things.

The first is that the blade angle is incorrect. This is controlled by the position of your rear wrist, which should be locked-in during setup. The second likely culprit is that your forward sweeping arm is pulling down rather than sweeping out. To avoid this, you have to consciously keep your forward arm pushed upward during the sweep to keep the blade on the surface. The last and most probable cause is the improper positioning of your rear arm and hand. Consider this hand as a point that is almost fixed in space, a stationary pivot that moves very little. The paddle sweeps around it while your body is lifted toward it. Hold that arm next to the boat, slightly bent, and high out of the water. Don't let it get pinned against the boat. When this happens, you restrict the sweep and cause the paddle to head downward rather than out.

You may not be able to integrate all of this into a functioning roll for quite some time. Learning to roll takes time and concentration. You can practice all of these, or any other instructions, perfectly and not get it. Rather than through action, you may be the sort who learns better by thinking things through. In quiet moments try to rehearse the motions of the roll in your mind and play with the mental exercise of envisioning yourself upside down.

If you can, get an instructor for rolling. Your life will be much easier for it. But if you can't, find a patient, caring soul who will help you through the roll. You'll need this person for your own safety and to point out the errors you can't see. Although your assistant need not even know what a kayak is, he or she must understand how to right one with you in it. When you are ready to be pulled up, give an agreed-on signal (for example, slap the hull three times) and go into a tight tuck, leaning forward, nose to the deck and arms near the side of the boat. Your helper should be standing to one side. He or she can then either reach over the bottom of or underneath the upturned kayak, grab the far cockpit coaming, gunwale, or your arm, and pull you up and over.

Some words about practicing: Go easy on yourself. Although it takes drive and determination during the stroke, you don't have to carry that attitude over to the whole project. Rest often, and make rolling sessions short to prevent dizzy spells. The human body isn't built for too much of this hanging-upside-down-with-water-in-the-nose stuff. At the least, wear a nose clip to minimize the discomfort. Better still, wear a diving mask to keep the water out and an eye on what you are doing. In the beginning, the more input for your soggy, upside-down brain, the better your chances of getting this thing right.

If you like, you can make your first attempts at a complete roll using the paddle float. Keep on practicing with the float until you get this assisted roll perfect. At that point you should have a good grasp of what you are doing and why it is happening. From there you have to make the switch over to something closer to reality and use the paddle without the float.

If you have been paddling with very narrow blades, you might want to make the transition from float to bare blade easier by using a wider blade for your rolling. Larger blades provide greater support, which therefore makes rolling easier. In this way you can proceed in gentle steps, going from the float to the large blade and finally to your own paddle. Or you can dive in and try your own right from the start.

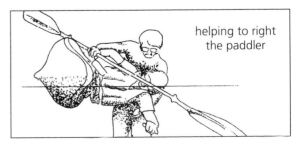

helping to right the paddler

REENTRY-AND-ROLL

Good seamanship is based on backups. If one thing doesn't work, have something else in your back pocket ready to go. The Eskimo roll should be your primary means of recovery from a capsize. But, no matter how much you've practiced, something may go wrong and you may not be able to roll up. In a wild predicament, fear might paralyze you and affect your ability to react, your rolling skills might be rusty, or a hundred other little things might keep you hanging upside down. When this happens, you'll need a backup. Whatever it is, it should leave you in a more stable position than you were in when you capsized.

One of the better backup recovery schemes is the previously explained paddle float reentry. Not everyone feels comfortable with it, nor is it always possible to use it in extreme conditions. In that case, you'll need another alternative, such as the reentry-and-roll.

The original reentry-and-roll technique was concocted to help kayakers who had either tried to roll, failed, and exited the boat, or had found themselves somehow washed out of the cockpit. The concept was to keep the boat inverted, reenter as if doing a wet exit in reverse, and then try to roll again. The idea worked in swimming pools but lacked a certain understanding of the realities. If you couldn't roll in the first place, how were you going to do it the second time, especially after all that mucking about under water?

Recently the technique has been modified to be more practical and forgiving of your errors; using a paddle float, you will now have a much better prospect of rolling up, and you will have a second chance that really means something.

After capsizing and either failing to roll or purposely exiting the boat, come to the surface. Leave the boat upside down and turn it so it is broadside to the waves with the side you normally set up on as the downwind side. (This is a spatially confusing concept in an inverted boat, worthy of a piece of tape on the setup side as a permanent reminder.) Get on the downwind side, extract your paddle float from its lashings, and place it on a blade.

Because your PFD will make you too buoyant to get under the boat, rotate the kayak halfway up on its side so you can get in. Your setup side should now be above the surface. Grab both sides of the coaming while holding the paddle on the side you

normally would set up on, with the paddle float forward. Now curl your legs in close to the body, get your feet into the cockpit, and pull yourself in. Once you're in, the boat may invert slightly without going all the way over, which is to your benefit. From this halfway-over position you can either try rolling or use a high brace to get yourself all the way up. The choice will depend on how you and your kayak sit in the water.

As soon as you are up, use the paddle float for support by jamming the paddle under the rigging on the rear deck; or, do an over-the-shoulder, one-handed sculling brace. Both of these methods will leave you with at least one hand free to bail and reseal the spray skirt. If there is proper flotation on board, especially in the form of watertight bulkheads, the accumulated water should be minimal.

Make no mistake about it, mastering the reentry-and-roll takes practice. Putting on a spray skirt with one hand in a rolling sea is nerve-wracking work, but it's worth it if this increases your defensive arsenal.

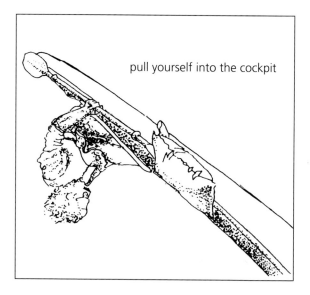

pull yourself into the cockpit

LAUNCHING

If it is at all possible, and most of the time it is, avoid surf. Plan your journeys so they begin and end in sheltered water. When paddling on bays and smaller lakes, this should pose no problem. But on larger lakes, or when cruising an ocean's outer coast, you may have no choice.

Given some experience and a highly maneuverable slalom whitewater kayak or a specialized surfing kayak, paddling in the surf can be a lot of fun. But sea kayaks are not built for this kind of stuff. They like to go straight and are reluctant to turn. Such traits are to your advantage once out in the open, but within the surfline they can mean some occasional excitement. If you can't avoid paddling through surf, or are perversely drawn to it, at least make sure your sea kayak is strongly built, has rugged foot braces, carries no deck cargo, is fitted with carrying toggles (not loops) at both ends, and has 100 percent failproof flotation.

If you must deal with surf, try to arrange things so you only encounter it on the way out. Going out through surf is a lot easier and safer than coming back through it. For one thing, you know exactly what you are getting into. When sitting offshore, beyond the surfline contemplating a landing, all you can see are the backs of the breakers. But from shore you can see the whole show. You are therefore afforded the luxury of being able to make a decision to go out or stay put, rather than being offshore and having no choice at all.

In very general terms there are two kinds of breakers: spilling breakers, which break with foam cascading down their face; and curling breakers, which curl over and dump their tops at the base. To put things more in your favor, seek out a beach with spilling breakers, which are products of a gently sloping bottom and which have less punch. These usually break away from the shore in multiple surflines with a lot of broken water ("soup") between them and the beach. Curling breakers are caused by bottoms that drop off or shelve steeply and generally break closer to shore in a single surfline.

If you've made the decision to head out, spend some time studying the surf from a high vantage point. Know what you are getting yourself into. Check the beach at low tide to see if there is anything beneath the surface, such as rocks, coral, or a steep drop-off, that could make things difficult. Notice how the surf breaks at both high and low tides; one is usually better than the other. Be aware of the direction and strength of the wind. Strong offshore (coming from the land) winds hold waves up and delay breaking or can even flatten them completely. Sea breezes push a messy chop ahead of them, generally increase throughout the day, and become still near dawn.

Take your time to look for patterns in the surf. You may find sections that, because of bottom contours, break differently from the rest of the beach. Rip currents, which are outbound streams of up to 5 knots, can be used for a free ride. You'll observe that the larger waves come in sets or a definable pattern. To decipher these sets or patterns, you may be able to count the waves or time the period between them, although neither will be absolutely accurate. Your best bet is to remember the pattern, recognizing how high the largest look and what comes before and after them. Get a feel for the surf. Try to envision a window of opportunity in which the waves are at their least powerful, with more green than white water inside the breakline. The idea is to launch your boat and be nearing the surfline after the largest wave of the set has spent itself. Be patient and wait.

Know the size of the waves you will encounter; anything over 6 feet should be your limit. You can judge the heights of waves by standing at water's edge. If the top of a breaking wave extends above the horizon line, it is higher than your eye level and thus is about 5½ feet high. To estimate smaller waves, kneel (about 4 feet) or sit (about 2½ feet). This is a reasonably accurate method, although waves somehow seem to be a lot larger when looming overhead.

To launch, place the kayak in the shallows or on the beach where the wash from the larger breakers can reach it. Point it directly into the waves. Get in and seal yourself up, and if you have a rudder, make sure it is raised so it does not get damaged in the shallow water. If you are on the beach, wait until the surge reaches you, then push down and hand-walk your way into the water until you are afloat. It may take a few waves to do this. When you are able to paddle, keep the bow pointed into the waves until you've built up some forward motion. If a small bit of soup grabs the bow obliquely before you are underway, it can swing the boat around and make it difficult, if not impossible, to get pointed back in the right direction. If you can, find a helper to give you a shove straight out or hold the bow until there's a lull and you can get going.

Once free of the beach, paddle with force and determination. Use short brisk strokes so you can react quickly to maintain your balance or alter direction. Your course is head-on, perpendicular to the waves. As you paddle out, try to pace yourself by holding back or sprinting to miss the worst of it. If you've timed it right and you are lucky, you'll be able to get outside the surfline without a major confrontation. As a wave approaches, whether it is broken whitewater or is still a swell, you'll get over it as long as you keep paddling. When it arrives, lean back to help lift the bow, and then lean forward as it passes, all the time aggressively paddling to attack the wave, clawing your way over.

There will be times when you're not so lucky, and you'll see that the wave is about to break right on you. If it is small, under 3 feet, keep your head down with your chin buried in your PFD. Time your strokes so that when the wave hits the bow, a paddle blade will be entering the solid part of the wave. As the wave reaches you, pull yourself through, letting the PFD take the impact. Do not stop paddling or hold your paddle up with the idea that the wave will pass around you. It will, but it will also wash you backward or smash the paddle's shaft back into you. Paddle through with force. If the wave is steep, you'll come flying out the back like a Polaris missile. It's a great rush, and it's perfectly permissible to whoop like mad while in flight.

If you've miscalculated the surf from the shore and are about to be pounded by something with genuine malicious intent, your response will have to become equally aggressive. When faced with a towering monster, dig in and paddle like someone possessed (with the will to live). The attack plan is to build up maximum momentum so you can punch through the wave. Keep your head down, so the water has less to grip on, and keep your weight forward. It is most important to avoid being hit in the upper body by the full force of the wave, which has the potential to drive you back or over and back.

Paddle on no matter what. As you emerge from the back of the wave, congratulate yourself, take a deep breath, and continue on with all haste out of the surfline. Keep up a steady pace until you are farther out than you would think necessary, otherwise a large set may come through and take you by surprise.

If you've miscalculated the size and power of the surf, you may have to adopt an even more defensive tactic. When surfers think they are about to get creamed by a wave, they flip over and let the bottom of the board take the brunt of it; meanwhile their bodies create enough drag to keep them from being swept back in. If the wave is less than 6 feet high and you have a failproof roll, you can do the same. Set up for the roll, capsize, keep your head well tucked in toward the deck for protection, hang in there while you feel you are going through the rinse cycle, and when the wave has passed, roll up. When back on the surface, paddle like crazy to get past the line of breakers.

Capsizing to protect yourself from curling breakers can be dangerous. In fact, paddling out through curling surf isn't too wise to begin with. There is a very real possibility of being flipped over backward and tossed around as if in a cocktail shaker. In these extreme situations, your only defense may be to capsize the boat, get out of it, and hold on to the bow toggle (never put your hand through the loop; if the boat rolls, it can trap and injure your arm). In this way, the boat precedes you as you are slowly dragged back toward the beach to rethink your options.

Meet breakers head-on.

LANDING

When confronted by breaking waves when returning home, prudent mariners from time immemorial have taken one of two approaches: go elsewhere or wait. Only the uninitiated, overconfident, or impatient would charge blindly into the breach, ignoring the precepts of discretion and sound judgment. It is no different for sea kayakers sitting beyond the surf, wondering what to do.

If you are thinking of landing through surf, consider option one and go elsewhere. In most cases surf is something that can be avoided. Plan ahead. Look for coves, points that stick out and create protected beaches, sheltering rocks, small islands, or a passage that bypasses the outer shore altogether.

Option two, waiting it out, is almost impossible for a kayaker. Wind and waves take a long time to change. But if there is absolutely nowhere else to go, you may have no choice, even if the surf looks or sounds threatening.

If you've estimated the waves to be no more than 6 feet high and there is a good landing spot on the beach, there is no reason why you shouldn't make it. Your first task is to learn what's waiting for you inside the surfline. Check your chart for bottom contours, determine if the beach is sand or rocks or if there are any obstructions just offshore. Stay away from swimmers. Once you've ascertained that you've found a likely spot, wait. Sit well outside the surfline and determine how close together the waves are and their speed, height, and steepness. Larger waves break farther out. Find where they break and paddle near. If it doesn't seem too bad, start looking for a pattern.

Waves conveniently organize themselves in sets, multiple wave systems superimposed on each other, as they near the shore. When the troughs of these patterns coincide, you get a lull; when the peaks come together, the surf becomes larger. Sets can be tracked by counting, by timing, or by simply remembering their pattern. You want to come in on the small ones that follow right after the largest waves of the set.

Your best plan of attack is to avoid being picked up by a wave and hurled shoreward. Surfing may be fun, but once underway you relinquish almost all command of your craft. To maintain some semblance of control, you want to paddle in under your own power on the back of a breaking wave.

It's a matter of timing. After you are positive that the last large wave has passed, paddle in toward shore where the smaller waves will break. Stay outside this breakline. As a small one comes in, paddle backward to prevent taking off when you feel the stern lift. As the stern starts to drop, the wave is passing and you should begin paddling for all you're worth. You want to be high up on the back of the wave so it will carry you along as it breaks in front of you. Do not get ahead of it or you'll go over the falls and start surfing. Don't lag too far behind or the countercurrent on the wave's back will hold you, increasing the chance of being overtaken by the next breaker.

Because your very best paddling speed is probably 5 knots, and the wave is traveling at double (or triple) that, you won't be able to hold on to one wave all the way in. Try to get through the main line of breakers. Once in the soup, you can surf in or paddle with an occasional back stroke as a holding action.

Another method of getting in under control is to come in backward. This technique gives you an out anytime you find things are not going well, making it perfect for landing on unknown beaches. However, it is not suitable for large surf (over 6 feet) or surf that breaks right on the shore.

Start by paddling in on the back of the last large wave of a set. Get in as far as you can and turn seaward before the next wave reaches you. If it is breaking, paddle toward it so you won't be swept backward. The larger the breaker, the harder you'll have to paddle to maintain your position. Between waves, paddle backward toward the beach. Like a

Follow in on the back of a wave.

boxer, you can bob, weave, parry, and thrust, maneuvering your way shoreward in safety. Do not use your rudder during this type of surf work. It is too vulnerable and easily broken or bent if it bounces along the bottom. Stick to the basics of paddling for steering.

If the breaker is small enough, and you're willing to forgo some control for a little adventure, you can surf in. Wait for a wave and paddle before it. Unless the surf is very small (under 2 feet) do not head straight in. Hard-to-turn boats such as sea kayaks have a tendency to rush down the wave's face and bury their noses (pearling). The wave then grabs the stern and slews it around (broaching); in big waves you can wind up standing on end (appropriately called an *endo*) with your stern in the air and a greatly diminished chance of coming down right side up.

As you gather speed, lean back to keep the bow up and slow yourself down. Using a stern rudder stroke on the side you wish to turn toward, head diagonally across the face of the wave. If you can, steer away from the whitewater where the wave has already broken. Because you are no longer on level water, lean in toward the wave to keep your balance. Leaning away from a wave will guarantee a capsize. If the wave is very steep, convert your stern rudder stroke to a low brace and lean on that. Eventually the part of the wave you are on will break. There will be a surge of power shoreward, which must be counteracted by aggressively leaning toward the wave while you support yourself with either a high or low brace depending on the wave's height. As you are swept along in this controlled broach, keep your arms close to your body and flexible to absorb the considerable buffeting. On smaller waves, plant the blade on the wave's back. When you can't reach over the wave, stick the paddle high up in the soup. You'll get a surprising amount of support, but little control over where you are going.

If you capsize, immediately lean forward and

Bracing on a breaking wave.

tuck in to protect your head. If you can, try to roll up. If you can't, get out of the kayak as soon as possible. Whether you've left the kayak on purpose or were washed out by a wave, your first objectives are to keep the boat upside down so it doesn't fill with water, and to stay seaward of the kayak so it doesn't get thrown into you. If the surf is moderate, you can hold onto an end of the kayak and let the waves push you in. Hold only the kayak itself or a toggle. Do not put your hand or fingers in a grab loop. A kayak rolling in the surf can turn these into twisting nooses that can entrap you. If the surf is not so moderate, get clear of the kayak as quickly as you can and swim in with the paddle.

Once you reach the shallows, get out and carry the boat above the waterline. In surf that breaks close to or directly on the shore, get the boat up on land as quickly as possible before the backwash sucks it out. While holding the boat in the wash, keep it end-on to the oncoming waves, otherwise you'll be chasing it up and down the beach and end up with banged shins.

The controlled broach.

1

2

3

4

INTO

On its own, wind is not much of a problem for sea kayaks. Its primary effect is seen in how the boat wants to situate itself in relation to the wind. This is called *weathercocking*, and each boat is different. Most kayaks want to point their bows into the wind while underway, making it very easy to paddle in that direction.

Waves are not so benign. Like big goons, they are there to do the wind's bidding. It takes time to get them going, but after being pushed by the wind for a while, they begin to follow its direction. The longer they're pushed, the meaner they get. Unless you kayak in a seismographically active area, almost all the waves you'll confront will have been created by the wind. This could be a wind that is ten miles away, or a thousand. Each wave is a composite, with its size determined by how long and how hard the wind has been blowing, and how far it has traveled.

Although waves are products of the bullying wind, they are also easily manipulated by other forces and factors. A current from either a river or a tide running against the wave pattern will cause them to steepen. Shallow underwater ledges or irregularities confuse them, narrow funnelling passages hasten them, points of land can bend them, and steep shorelines can bounce them around. Because of the diminutive size of our vessels, even small wave patterns can be a challenge. But the contest is not one-sided. Given the proven seaworthiness of a skillfully handled sea kayak, you can come out on top if you go at it with an aggressive attitude. Attack waves. Lean into and push toward them. By taking the offensive, you can often bully them right back.

If you are paddling into the wind when there is little wave buildup, your main problem will be stamina—having enough strength to keep going. A strong headwind can easily cut 2 or more knots from your speed. At a cruising speed of 3 to 4 knots, losing 2 knots is a major setback. All you can do is reconcile yourself to it and keep moving as fast as you can. Find a paddling rhythm with a strong stroke that can be maintained, then dig in. Put full body twist into it and push with the recovering arm, but be careful of wrist strain. Ease your stroke dur-

ing gusts; paddle with just enough pressure to keep the boat moving.

How much wind is too much? In protected waters where waves are not a significant factor, a beginner should have no trouble in winds up to 12 knots. From 20 knots on, even protected bodies of water will be affected by the wind and should be left to more experienced kayakers. Somewhere around 30 knots is the maximum limit for almost everyone; progress into it will border on impossible.

On open water, the game changes because waves become part of the equation. In light winds, the waves are just enough to make paddling interesting. Your kayak will feel alive, there's some spray flying, and the waves rushing toward you make it feel as if you are going much faster than you are. As the wind picks up, so will the waves. For smaller waves, time your strokes so the paddle enters an oncoming wave and begin pulling back as the crest arrives. For larger waves, paddle hard on the downward slope and ease off on the upward slope. Widely spaced, deep-water swells are easiest, because they gently undulate past. More troublesome is the short chop found in shallow waters that have recently been whipped up. The boat can plough into these short-period waves; this can be alleviated by shifting your load or leaning back to lighten the bow. Turning in waves is difficult and is best done on wave tops. This gets the boat's ends out of the water, making turning easier.

Paddling into wind and waves forces you to expend a great deal of energy on propulsion, yet a minimum on balancing. Going to windward may be hard work, but it has the advantage of being the least vulnerable course because it is much harder for a wave to knock you end-over-end than it is for it to roll you over on your side. Also, waves are psychologically less threatening if you can see them coming, rather than having them sneak up from behind or from your side. When things get out of control, or you need to take a break, head into the wind and hold your position with a slow, forward stroke. This is the rough-water way of putting the boat in neutral.

ACROSS

Sea kayaks are at their most awkward when wind or waves are coming across the bow. It's part of their nature, something that can't be avoided but nevertheless can be dealt with.

With the wind on your side (beam), the kayak's desire to weathercock can become a demanding nuisance. Very few, if any, kayaks are neutrally balanced to the wind. Almost all want to veer off in one direction or the other, and to varying degrees. Most boats, if they weathercock at all, do so to windward. This means that the farther away from paddling directly into the wind your course takes you (unless you're paddling almost directly downwind), the more the boat will want to turn into the wind.

In gentle winds, carved turning may be sufficient to hold your course without sacrificing forward speed. Edging (tilting) the boat toward the wind will tend to head it downwind. Plus, with the boat on an angle, your stroke automatically becomes wider on the lower (windward) side, helping to keep the bow away from the wind. If this isn't having the desired effect, the next step is to broaden the sweep of your stroke. If that doesn't do it, shift your grip a few inches up the shaft to increase your leverage on the sweeping side.

Another way of handling weathercocking is to alter the boat's underwater profile by adding more area aft. If your boat is equipped with one, lowering the skeg will help balance its steering and may prevent the stern from swinging downwind and the bow from pointing up. If you have a rudder, lower it and keep it centered. As the wind increases you will have to begin compensating with the rudder. You'll find that as long as you are moving, the rudder need only be turned a few degrees to neutralize the most severe weathercocking. Your paddling style and rhythm will not be affected and you can make good progress.

As the wind gets stronger, keep your arms and stroke lower. This increases the bracing component of the stroke and prevents a gust from getting hold of the windward blade on its return stroke (which is more likely with a feathered than a nonfeathered paddle). If the wind hits your blade and wants to carry it away, don't fight it. Release your grip on the windward side and let the paddle go where it may. Holding on can put you off balance and increase the chance of capsizing. Just let it go, then bring it back at a lower shaft angle and resume paddling with some extra caution.

As the wind builds, so will the waves, increasing the probability of being knocked over. To the edging (tilting the kayak) that you are already doing for the carved turn, you will now have to add some leaning (tilting the body) to help counteract the lateral capsizing potential of the waves and to resist the wind. As when paddling into the waves, here, too, you have to take an aggressive stance and always lean toward them. The larger and steeper they are, the more you have to lean. Do this by adding a bracing blade angle to your stroke for support and forward propulsion without letting it hinder your cadence.

The only thing that should interrupt your pace are waves so large or steep that they become threatening. Your only defense will be to break stride and brace. Depending on the wave's size, go into a high or low brace. As the wave hits, lean into it and sustain the brace until it passes. Another tactic is to turn into the big ones so you take them bow-on. This only works if you can turn your boat easily and quickly, which may be difficult in a beam sea. If a few forward sweeps on the downwind side won't turn you, try three or four reverse sweep strokes on the windward side. These may slow the boat down but offer a more powerful turning force. You may find it impossible to turn your boat when it is in a trough with the ends trapped between two waves. If so, wait until the boat rises to the top of a wave, which will reduce its immersed length, then try to turn.

While all this is going on, and you're concentrating on just making forward progress in the right direction without losing your balance, you are simultaneously being blown sideways with the wind. Make allowances for this drift. Line up two landmarks to act as reference points to see just how much you are drifting off course.

WITH

Finally! Here's a course where you can lighten up and let the wind do some of the work, right? Well, yes, but it's not quite that simple.

When the wind is light, under 10 or 15 knots, your only concern may be some mild weathercocking. If you are heading exactly in the direction of the wind, it won't have any effect other than to push you along your way. But as soon as you let the wind get even the slightest bit to one side, it's going to try to swing you around. When this happens, minor course-correcting strokes should be all that is needed to keep you headed in the right direction. A forward sweep stroke ending in a stern rudder should do it. Just don't let the boat yaw too far off course before making your correction.

The deceiving part about downwind travel is that because you are moving with it, the wind never seems as strong as it really is. But there's always that moment of surprise when you stop, or turn into the wind, and find that what you thought was a nice cruising breeze is, in fact, a nasty blow. Keep an eye on the waves. If they have grown to the point where you have to fight to keep from broaching, you've let things go too far.

Before that, as the waves are building, you will find yourself hitching rides and gaining ground with each wave. At this stage they have grown to where their internal motion alternately pushes you ahead and holds you back. The water in the crests moves with the wave, and the water in the troughs moves against it. To use this to your advantage, paddle a little faster as your stern lifts to the oncoming wave. When you

feel yourself accelerating, paddle even harder. If the waves are the right size, you may even surf for a short distance. As the crest passes and your bow lifts, the forward push is over. Once in the trough, strong paddling will do you no good, so stroke only to keep from being drawn back. As the next wave approaches, the cycle starts over again. In this manner your progress will increase with a noticeable decrease in effort. Get attuned to the wave pattern so there is no need to put yourself off balance by continually looking over your shoulder to see what's coming. Feel what the waves are doing and let yourself go with them.

As the wind and waves build, you may find your downwave speeds increasing at an alarming rate. These rapid accelerations are akin to surfing, with all its inherent dangers. Your main concern now is not making progress but retaining control. After you have been picked up by a wave and are running with it, use a stern rudder stroke to manage direction, being ready to convert it into a low brace if you veer too far off and begin to broach. If you feel you are no longer in total control, or frequently come close to broaching, it is time to stop surfing and begin slowing down. To reduce the likelihood of taking off, stop paddling as the wave builds up behind you. Or, you can back-paddle to brake, letting the crests pass by completely. Although you may feel you are lagging behind by doing this, you are still being blown downwind and making reasonable time. An alternative for really big swells is to turn into the waves and let yourself be blown backward while holding your bow to the wind and waves.

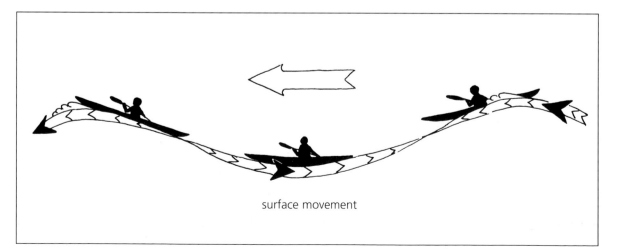

surface movement

TWO OR MORE

So far everything you have read in this book assumes that you will be on your own. This is not only the most direct method of learning sea kayaking, it is also an essential attitude. You are participating in an activity with risks. And whether you are on your own or with others, the risks of your journey are ultimately borne by you and you alone.

However, there is that old saying about safety in numbers. Don't believe it for a minute, or doubt it for a second. No matter how big a crowd you have around you, in the end you are on your own; but if you can, never forgo the company of others on the water. It is not that it is unsafe to paddle alone, its just that it is much safer if you are not. Once away from land, a group becomes a team, a team whose purpose is added security, plus (and this should never be discounted) the pleasure and support of companionship in an alien environment.

As soon as someone joins you, a team is formed. With a partner along there is help for rescues and aid nearby. But if something really goes wrong, it can happen to two as well as to one, or if it only happens to one, the other may not be able to handle it. With three, everyone's chances greatly improve. It is an axiom of life that, although it may take only one person to get into trouble, it usually takes several more to get out. Three boats now offer two to help the one; or, one to help and the other to go for assistance. The odds are improved with three and stay that way until you reach six, with eight being the upper limit. Above this the numbers become unwieldy with too many people to be looked after or to look after others, so smaller subgroups should be formed.

Groups, as well as a lone traveler, can add an extra measure of safety to their trip by notifying a responsible person on shore of the proposed cruise. This "float plan" should include time of departure, expected route, stopping points, final destination, and estimated time of arrival. On longer trips you might contact the coast guard or marine police and let them know what you're doing, when you'll be back, and the name of your home contact. Don't count on the coast guard to initiate a search, though; it's not their job to keep track of every group that ventures out on the water. Be sure your home contact has the number of the local coast guard station, so if you don't come back according to schedule, your contact can notify the coast guard to request a search.

Without a doubt it is safer to cruise in a group, but never be lulled into a false sense of security just because you are surrounded by others. Although they can help, stand by you, and get you through situations that you might not have been able to cope with on your own, you should still, in the end, consider yourself to be responsible for your own actions.

MANAGEMENT AND COMMUNICATION

Of necessity there must be group management. This is made easier if everyone shares a common goal, is of relatively equal skills, and there is only one leader. However, the leader should not be an all-powerful monarch. He or she should be the group's mediator, the one experienced person designated to make decisions in moments of mass indecision. As much as possible all issues should be resolved while still on shore: leaders chosen, routes and meeting or stopping points determined, communications set and understood, weaknesses and strengths acknowledged.

The logistics of group travel are more clear-cut. In launching through surf, the leader (chosen because of experience) helps the others and collects them if something goes wrong. When the others are safely beyond the breakers, the leader joins them. In landing, the order is reversed. The leader heads in and secures the beach, directing the others through the surf. The others should come in one at a time while watching the leader's hand signals (for example, arms held vertically means go straight, arms held out to the sides means stop, arms pointing to either side show the preferred direction).

On the water the group can gather in a loose formation. For three boats keep one ahead and two behind, one on each quarter. Larger groups will not stay tightly formed, and the leader is best off to the side or moving freely through the group like a sheep dog. In addition to a leader, groups larger than three should have a point person, someone familiar with the route who sets the pace. The strongest or most experienced kayaker should pull up the rear as a sweep to help and encourage weaker paddlers. Within the group, paddlers should pair off to keep track of and support each other. All paddlers must know the course and cruising plan, but none should set off alone. To do so subverts the group's security. To add equality and variety and to help morale, responsibilities can be rotated during a cruise. Or, if this all sounds too structured, the group can forget the above and travel as an informal pack. As long as everyone can watch out for each other, the results will be the same.

Maintaining boat spacing is difficult over long stretches of open water. Try to keep boats close enough to communicate but not so close that they cannot maneuver. A good standard is two or three boat lengths between kayaks. Stay within hailing (yelling) distance of each other if possible. If it gets rough, close up ranks. Voice communication may be impossible in even moderate winds, and visual contact may be difficult if seas are over 3 feet because members of the group become hidden in the troughs. In these cases air horns can be used, because the sound of whistles does not carry in windy conditions. A good code is one blast for attention, two for assembly, and three for an emergency. Hand signals similar to those used for surf landings can also be used. When one paddler sees the signal of another, that paddler should also signal. Thus the message gets relayed quickly throughout the group. Signals must be kept simple and easily understood. At night, both sound and light signals can be used. Be sure to practice or test communication systems in a variety of conditions; it is very hard for a group of kayakers to keep in touch even in good conditions.

Group decisions should be based on the performance of the least experienced or weakest paddler. This can be frustrating to the more advanced but should be enforced. Do not encourage the less experienced to push their limits just so they will not hold you back. To do so invites disaster. Ideally, everyone in the group should be capable of rescuing others and responsible for his or her own emergency, navigation, and rescue gear as well. Discuss and, if possible, rehearse rescue procedures before leaving.

When emergencies such as a capsize or gear failure occur, the two closest boats should assist while the others stay together and hold their positions nearby but not so close as to add to the problem.

Rafting is an ideal method for resting, eating, making repairs, or discussing matters without having to continually paddle to hold your position. To raft, come abreast of another kayak so you are both facing in the same direction and bridge the two boats with your paddles. In this way the two kayaks become a wide, flexible, and very stable raft. More boats can be added to the raft as desired.

ASSISTED RESCUES

There are two types of situations in which even the most experienced solitary paddlers will not be able to rescue themselves. One is when they can no longer propel their craft; the other, being the worst of all circumstances, is when they have become separated from their kayak while far from shore. Neither is an admirable position to be in, and both absolutely require outside assistance.

When a paddler can no longer propel the kayak—for example, a paddle breaks and the spare was somehow lost, a wrist is injured, illness hits— then the disabled paddler should be towed. If a boat has been properly set up, the predicament is merely a change in plans, not a disaster. What is necessary is a bow line rigged, or a special line stowed and ready for this purpose.

The disabled kayak will most likely be drifting broadside to the wind. Approach from the windward side to set up the towline. The line attached to the towing boat must be done in such a way that it can easily be made secure, immediately freed, and will not foul deck gear. A quick-release fitting (such as a cam cleat), can be permanently bolted in place behind and off to one side of the cockpit. An alternative is for the towing paddler to hold the rope. Yet another way is to tie a bowline in the end of the towline and put one arm through the loop so it rests over your shoulder. To get free, let go of the paddle on that side and let the line slip down your arm. There are numerous ready-made towing systems available at kayaking stores. To make life a little easier, keep the towline two or three boat lengths long,

especially in following seas, with one boat length as a minimum.

Worse than not being able to continue on your own is to find yourself separated from your boat. It is probably the most demoralizing situation a kayaker could experience. Even a small lake becomes ominously large, the now former paddler dwarfed and defenseless. It has been sadly recorded how drowning victims believed that shore looked closer than it actually was. If your kayak has gone down or been blown away, don't try to swim for it. Immediately signal your comrades for help.

The first priority is to get the swimmer out of the water to reduce the risk of exposure (hypothermia), which is the greatest disabler and killer of kayakers. The rescuing kayaker should turn into the wind and hold position. The swimmer then crawls onto the aft deck, staying face down, as low as possible, with legs spread for stability, holding on to the waist of the paddler. For short distances, such as bringing the swimmer to his or her kayak or a nearby shore, the swimmer can hang off the bow with legs and arms wrapped around the hull, head off to one side. Just be aware that your boat will handle drastically differently with a person hanging off or on top of it.

Swimmer rescues and towing can and should be practiced. Emergencies will always throw in the unexpected, and no one technique or method will always work.

ASSISTED REENTRY

Nothing is quite so desperate as a lone paddler swimming next to a capsized kayak. Even in calm conditions the feeling of being totally cut off is demoralizing enough to induce panic. At a time like this having the support of others becomes invaluable. You may have your paddle float reentry down pat and may have practiced rolling until you're dizzy, but one day it may all fall apart and your only recourse will be an assisted reentry.

In a group situation, an assisted reentry is easier and faster than trying to do it on your own. Climbing back on board while somebody steadies the kayak makes it more likely that you will be able to get yourself together and on your way with less hassle or wasted effort. In most cases the assisted reentry is the most reliable rescue there is. But, as with everything else, you should know the drill and have practiced it before it's ever needed so a capsize and subsequent rescue becomes only a minor annoyance, not high drama at sea.

On being called to help, get to the downed kayaker as soon as possible. The preferred setup is to be on the windward side of the boat with both bows pointing in the same direction. But don't waste too much time maneuvering about. If it's faster to be on the downwind side with the boats pointing in opposite directions, do it. This procedure will work either way.

When the two boats are together, the person in the water should right the capsized kayak. Do not bother bailing it out just yet. Take both paddles and lay them across the boats directly behind the cockpits. Or, if the boats are pointing in opposite directions, place the paddles behind the coaming of the rescuing boat and in front of the coaming of the boat being rescued. The rescuing kayaker then leans over, puts the closest arm under the paddles, between the boats, and reaches forward to grab the other boat's coaming. The paddle shafts are now trapped under the rescuer's armpit and pressing down on both decks. The rescuer's weight is on the paddles, not on his or her arms. The forward hand can be used to steady the boats by holding the other's coaming or, because that hand is not bearing any weight, held out to help the paddler being rescued.

The person in the water stays even with the cockpit, grabs hold of the extending paddles with one hand, the coaming of his or her kayak with the other, and crawls onto the aft deck facing astern. Staying as low as possible, with most of his or her weight toward the rescuing boat and the rescuer counterbalancing any movements, the person being rescued works his or her legs into the cockpit, turns over, and slithers down onto the seat. Once in, the rescuing kayaker should continue holding on until the one being rescued has bailed the boat, resecured the spray skirt, and feels ready to go on.

A modification to the above technique is to use a continuous loop of rope or nylon webbing as a sling to help get back in. It is more than likely that part of the reason you wound up in the water was because you were too tired to react properly. Although the standard assisted reentry is easier than a self-rescue, it still takes a good amount of effort to haul yourself up and into the boat, an effort you might not be capable of. A sling eases that job by letting you use your more powerful leg muscles to push, rather than only using your arms to pull.

The sling is wrapped around the cockpit coaming and is long enough to hang off the side like a stirrup just below the bottom of the boat. You then put one foot in the sling and push yourself up onto the kayak while your rescuer steadies your boat. Slings must be accurately measured, tied, and tested ahead of time, then stowed in a spot that will be convenient when you are in the water.

A final word about rescues: there may come a time when conditions are so dangerous that the best way to save someone is by not trying to rescue them. That is, you make the decision that even an assisted rescue is not possible—and may result in injury to others—and you must resort to outside resources. But I know that this is unlikely to ever happen to you because, through good judgment and seamanship, you will not let yourself get into that sort of desperate situation in the first place.

Assisted reentry.

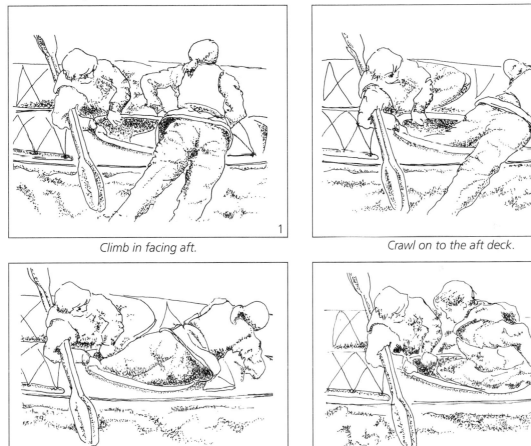

1	2
Climb in facing aft.	*Crawl on to the aft deck.*
3	4
Place legs in cockpit.	*Turn over and slide in.*

CONTINUING EDUCATION

As a prudent mariner you must take full responsibility for your actions and be proficient in and constantly perfecting the basic arts of sea kayaking. That's what the following section aims to help you do by continuing your sea kayaking education.

By now you have a vessel that is sturdy, well equipped, fits like a glove, has full flotation, and is supplied with the necessary safety gear. You are properly clothed for paddling or immersion. You know how to paddle comfortably and with strength for long periods, are well-versed in maneuvering your craft, have a feel for balance, maintain a well-practiced repertoire of brace strokes, are able to do an Eskimo roll, and know one or more methods of self- and assisted-rescue.

Now you are ready to further prepare yourself with a few well-chosen and regularly practiced conditioning and limbering exercises, and to learn to deal with common kayaker maladies and dangers such as tendonitis, seasickness, over-exposure to the sun, and hypothermia. Finally, you will work on developing a firm understanding of navigation and weather and become fluent in reading the environment around you.

Think of this next section as graduate school. These are not electives; these lessons are the next step up in the education of the prepared kayaker.

Another step in the continuing education of the sea kayaker is finding and using other resources. The last pages of this book show you how to find schools, clubs, symposia, and other resources for adding to your skills as well as meeting fellow kayakers. There's also a bibliography of the best books on kayaking, seamanship, boats and gear, and camping, as well as tips for disabled paddlers and for families wishing to voyage together.

This is both the end and the beginning. The foundations are built (basic paddling skills and sound equipment), and the walls and the roof are in place (rescue and recovery skills). Now it's time to refine the details that will start you on a lifetime of adventure.

BODY BASICS

CARE AND PREVENTION

Exercises

Think you're ready to head off toward the watery horizon? Well, not quite. An important bit of preparation for any sea kayaking trip, be it a day or a week, is exercise, both the long-term kind and the right-before-you-leave kind. If you're tempted to just "get in shape on the water," remember that one minor injury—a strained back or shoulder—can put you out of commission for weeks, and that such injuries can be avoided with just minor regular exercise. Even brisk walking, hiking, or running a few times a week is much better than nothing at all. And if you can't bring yourself to do some stretching at the dock, at least warm up by paddling slowly and gently and doing some gentle torso twists and hamstring stretches during your first half hour out in the boat.

A lot of beginning kayakers, in their newly acquired zeal for the sport, rush out and buy a rowing machine as their answer to the question "How do I train for kayaking?" A rowing machine might be a good addition to a complete training program, but it shouldn't be the only element. Consider that you use much more than just your legs and arms for kayaking: your lower back, abdomen, thighs, wrists, and even your ankles do more work than they may be accustomed to.

One of the easiest ways to acquire all-around fitness—and it's fun to boot—is to run an exercise course regularly. These courses are mapped, several miles long, and sprinkled with a dozen or more exercise stations: from stretching of hamstrings, arms, and back, to jumping jacks, pull-ups, push-ups, vaulting, and tummy crunches. Courses such as these emphasize low-impact activities, and usually have posted charts of recommended repetitions for beginner, intermediate, and expert levels, as well as target heart rates. In this way you condition a full range of muscle groups as well as gain cardiovascular fitness.

For pretrip stretching to warm up your muscles and reduce the chance for injury, or after you've done a long day's paddle, try these simple stretches. As with all exercises, do these stretches gently and fluidly, without bouncing or forcing your body to go farther than it wants.

- **Torso.** Sit on the ground with your legs positioned as they are in your boat. Holding your paddle in front of your chest, arms bent slightly, twist to one side and hold for a count of 20 seconds, then twist to the other side. Repeat two to three times.
- **Ankles.** Seated as for the torso twist, reach forward and grab one ankle with one hand while pulling back on the ball of that foot with the other hand; hold this stretch for a count of 20 seconds, then slowly rotate the foot to the right, left, and forward. Repeat with the other ankle.
- **Hamstrings.** Seated as for the torso twist and ankle stretch, slowly lean forward, reaching with your paddle toward your ankles, and hold for a count of 20 seconds, then slowly sit back up. Repeat two or three times (be gentle!).
- **Lower back.** Stand with your feet shoulder-width apart, knees slightly bent, lean forward and let your head and arms dangle down toward the ground, holding for a count of 20 seconds, then raise back up straight very slowly.
- **Wrists.** Gently pull the fingers of one hand back toward the forearm and hold for a count of 20 seconds, then reverse and pull them down toward the forearm, and repeat.

Holding your paddle squared to the shoulders, twist slowly to one side and then to the other to stretch your torso and hips.

Sitting in your boat or on land, lean forward and gently stretch your hamstrings.

Carefully stretch the wrists in both direction before, during, and after paddling.

Fuel and Hydration

The next step toward good health at sea is properly fueling and watering your body. In fact, drinking enough water, and, to a lesser degree, eating the right foods to provide your muscles with the right fuel, should be right up there with your paddle float and PFD as part of your safety gear. Time and again, even experienced paddlers don't drink enough or eat right and end up tired and dehydrated. At the least you can get a bad headache; at the worst dangerously exhausted and disoriented.

Sea kayakers are notorious for not drinking enough water. To make sure you hydrate your body sufficiently, tuck a couple of bottles of water on either side of your seat, or buy one of those neat hydration systems with a tube that you can use to access water on-the-go. . Drink often; if your urine is dark or you're not urinating as frequently as usual, you aren't drinking enough. To be sure, peeing at sea is not easy. Men can use a bailer or a plastic bottle. For women, there are devices such as the Freshette that give some freedom similiar to that enjoyed by men. But don't slack off on drinking because you don't want to go through the hassle of peeing.

Obviously, diet is important, too. Because alcohol and caffeine are diuretics (making you pee more and thus lose precious water), you should avoid them when kayaking. If you can't give them up, at least eat a sensible diet, the usual moderate-fat, high-carbohydrate dishes recommended for all athletes. On day-long paddles, take along some fast-energy snacks such as energy bars or fruit. Even a plain old candy bar is better than nothing. Actually, some tests have shown that a Snickers bar has energy-boosting and nutrition profiles similar to those of the leading (and more expensive) energy bars.

CAMELBAK

Tendonitis

Repetitive stress injuries, especially those to hands and arms, are common these days, especially in jobs that require a lot of keyboarding. But kayakers also need to be aware of wrist injuries. commonly grouped under the general term *tendonitis*, these problems manifest themselves as a pain on the side of the wrist and forearm just above the thumb, sometimes accompanied by a grating feeling or squeaking sound when the wrist is moved. The wrist tendons can become inflamed with overuse; in extreme cases scar tissue can develop, requiring surgery.

If you do develop persistent pain in the wrist during or after kayaking, you should consult a physician. In the meantime, you can perform this simple self-diagnostic test. Bend your thumb into the palm of your hand and grasp the thumb with your fingers; then bend your wrist back. If there is pain in the tendons to the thumb, you may have developed tendonitis.

To help prevent tendonitis, concentrate on varying the motion of your wrists; also do frequent stretching and flexing exercises. Don't push yourself to paddle all day if your wrists—or any other parts of you—are feeling strained, take frequent rest breaks or change your itinerary to a nearer destination. Rest for a day or two in between practice sessions.

If you do develop tendonitis, you can treat simple inflammation with cool compresses and anti-inflammatory medications such as ibuprofen, aspirin, or naproxen, and plenty of rest (no kayaking) until the inflammation is gone. If you do not treat tendonitis at the onset, scar tissue may develop, and months of pain, inactivity, and, possibly, surgery will be the result.

Sea Sickness

If you are prone to sea sickness in larger boats and are afraid to try sea kayaking because of that, try a test paddle. Even for people who commonly get ill on ferries or fishing boats, it is unlikely you'll experience the same malady in a sea kayak, because you're close to the water and the normal heaving and pitching that disorients the inner ear and cause nausea are generally absent in kayaking.

Just the same, it's a good idea to avoid fixating on your bow while paddling. Your normal routine of alert paddling—looking around you and watching for dangers such as approaching boats or wakes—will keep your mind centered well away from your boat. Situations with a higher risk of sea sickness while kayaking are when you pause for a long period in a heaving swell, especially if you are looking down at a chart, or if you are in really confused seas and your boat is being tossed violently about. Both are good indicators that it's time to get off the ocean, anyway. If you do get queasy, breathe deeply and concentrate on the horizon and your paddling.

As a precaution, you could try accupressure wrist bands (if your local kayak shop doesn't carry them, try a boating or scuba store), which some people claim work wonders to dispel sea sickness. Most over-the-counter medications will make you drowsy and impair your sense of balance. The one exception is meclizine (Bonine), which has minimal side effects.

Hypothermia

When your body can no longer keep warm, your core temperature drops, and you experience hypothermia. Many kayakers assume that hypothermia is a risk only if you are immersed in cold water for an extended period, but it can also build up over the course of a day, such as when you paddle for hours in sleet wearing inadequate clothing, especially if you haven't eaten properly. Hypothermia is a dangerous condition that must be remedied quickly.

The greatest danger of hypothermia is that once it begins, your mind has already become groggy

enough that subsequent decisions might be the wrong ones and could get you into more trouble. Mild hypothermia begins with shivering, stiffness, lethargy, and irritability. As it progresses, the skin begins to cool down and turn pale, because the body is shutting down circulation in its extremities to save its core. Disorientation, lack of coordination, and collapse are the signs of severe hypothermia.

If you or someone in your group begins to show signs of even mild hypothermia or is wet from immersion in cold water, paddle to shore immediately. Pitch a tent if possible, and put the person inside in a sleeping bag, preferably along with someone else for extra warmth. Replace all wet clothing and feed the victim hot liquids and food.

Never rub the skin of a hypothermia victim; this will stimulate blood flow to the skin and away from the body's core. Don't apply alcohol to the skin for the same reason. You can apply warm towels to the chest, neck, abdomen, and groin, but not the limbs (again, this will cause core cooling). If the victim does not improve within an hour, seek help.

Obviously the best thing is to avoid hypothermia. Dress for the water and for the weather, minimize time spent in the water by honing rescue skills, and don't wait until you're uncomfortably cold to add more clothing—it might be too late. Always carry spare clothes in cold conditions. If you are traveling far, bring along a stove, fuel, and adequate shelter. Eat properly by increasing your fat intake.

WEATHER WISE

Sea kayakers are slaves to the weather. No other water sport is more dominated by it—even sailboats aren't as affected as kayaks. Size alone lets them overcome obstacles that would stop a kayak dead in the water.

The scale of a sea kayak to its environment makes it that much more sensitive to what goes on around it. Next time you're paddling with someone, spend a moment to watch how that person's boat slices through the water. If you can let your imagination go for a second, you'll see a scaled-down ship on scaled-down waves. A sea kayak is but a tiny ship to which a 3-foot wave is analogous to a giant North Atlantic roller to an ocean liner. Likewise, a 10-knot breeze wouldn't be felt by the big ship, but it will have a significant effect on the progress of the kayak.

Sea kayakers should not only be interested in the weather in general, but also in the weather specific to the small world in which you are paddling. That is, you've got to learn how to interpret both the general weather patterns and, more importantly, what is coming at you from the horizon—your immediate weather patterns.

For collecting general weather information, your best sources are the dedicated weather channels on your VHF radio, the weather report on your local TV news program, or an inexpensive specialty radio that only receives weather broadcasts.

VHF radios have frequencies preset to get reports from the National Weather Service in the United States and from the coast guard in Canada. These frequencies are designated as channels WX 1, WX-2, and WX-3 in the United States, with an additional WX-4 in Canada. Each channel receives weather broadcasts from a local weather-service station. Depending on your location and your radio's strength, you will receive broadcasts from different weather stations on different channels. In this way you can build up a fair image of the general weather pattern.

To do this you must be able to understand the language of these reports. When they say that winds are light and variable, it means that the wind has a speed of 4 knots or less and varies in direction. A *small craft advisory* means winds of 18 to 33 knots, and a *gale*

warning is for winds from 34 to 47 knots, but these ratings should only be of academic interest to sea kayakers, because you should be safely off the water long before even small craft advisories go out.

Before you leave on your trip, you can also catch the most recent radar pictures of your area on television (the Weather Channel), or via the Internet from sources such as the National Oceanic and Atmospheric Administration (NOAA, pronounced "Noah") and the National Weather Service. Radar is a wonderful thing because it shows where concentrated cells of bad weather are located and in what direction they are moving, all within a relatively small sector.

When you are completely out of touch with any of these electronic marvels, you'll have to depend on your own observations to forecast general weather patterns. If you are untutored in meteorology, this may seem an almost impossible task. But if you can tell which direction the wind is coming from and read a barometer, you can make some surprisingly accurate forecasts using the table that follows.

The table on page 124 represents a composite of long-term observations for weather behavior throughout most of the continental United States and lower Canada. Its reliability diminishes below 30 degrees and above 50 degrees north latitude. There is nothing mysterious about it, and, with a little studying of basic weather, you'll see that it directly relates to typical patterns associated with areas of high and low pressure. These pressure changes are measured by a barometer, which should be consulted every three hours during the day to ascertain pressure trends. A compact combination altimeter-barometer, available through camping or mountaineering supply sources, can be conveniently carried with you. Be sure to follow the instructions carefully on how to calibrate and read your instrument.

There may be times when it seems that you have nothing at all to guide your forecasts; no radio, TV, barometer, or tables. Or you may need to shift from a more generalized forecast to a highly localized one for your paddling area. When this happens, you will have to depend on your own capabilities. Even if you don't know an isobar from a juice bar, it's easy to do if you are willing to let yourself tune in and really see what's around you.

Because they are moving at 3 knots inches away from the water's surface and repeating a simple relaxing motion for long periods, paddlers have plenty of time to absorb what is going on around them. In your daily routine, the patterns and effects of the atmosphere are there but often seem inconsequential or go unnoticed altogether. Once you come in direct contact with the world, as you do in a kayak, you get closer to feeling the environment, as our predecessors did, when there were no "official" weather reports, and people looked around them, heard, felt, or saw signs that they could read as nature's weather reports. These observations got handed down as folk sayings: some quite fanciful, others based on hard facts of empirically gained knowledge.

Weather Forecaster

By entering in the wind direction as you observe it, and the trend of the barometer for the preceding 3 hours, you can arrive at a fair estimate of the coming weather. This chart is intended for use in continental North America between 30 and 50 degrees north latitude. Barometric readings are in inches of mercury.

Wind	Barometer	Forecast
SW to NW	30.1 to 30.2, steady	Fair with slight temperature changes for 24 to 48 hours
SW to NW	30.1 to 30.2, rising rapidly	Fair followed by rain within 48 hours
SW to NW	30.2 and above, stationary	Continued fair with no major temperature changes
SW to NW	30.2 and above, falling slowly	Slowly rising temperature and fair for 48 hours
S to SE	30.1 to 30.2, falling slowly	Rain within 24 hours
S to SE	30.1 to 30.2, falling rapidly	Increasing wind and rain within 12 to 24 hours
SE to NE	30.1 to 30.2, falling slowly	Rain within 12 to 18 hours
SE to NE	30.1 to 30.2, falling rapidly	Increasing wind and rain within 12 hours
E to NE	30.1 and above, falling slowly	Summer: If winds are light, no rain for several days Winter: Rain within 24 hours
E to NE	30.1 and above, falling fast	Summer: Rain probably within 12 hours Winter: Rain or snow with increasing winds
SE to NE	30.0 or below, falling slowly	Rain will continue for 24 to 48 hours
SE to NE	30.0 or below, falling rapidly	Rain with high winds followed within 36 hours by clearing and colder in the winter
S to SW	30.0 or below, rising slowly	Clearing in a few hours and fair for several days
S to E	29.8 or below, falling rapidly	Severe storm imminent, followed by clearing within 24 hours and colder in winter
E to N	29.8 or below, falling rapidly	Summer: Severe NE gale and heavy rains Winter: Heavy snow and cold wave
Going to W	21.8 or below, rising rapidly	Clearing and colder in the winter

- The most famous bit of weather lore is one of proven worth and was spoken by Christ in Matthew 16:2–3: "When it is evening, ye say, it will be fair weather: for the sky is red. And in the morning, it will be foul weather today: for the sky is red and lowering." The old "red sky at night, sailor's delight," works. Most weather travels from west to east. If the setting sun were seen through the dust of dry air, it would appear red and fair, dry weather would arrive the next day.

- If you wake up to find that there is dew, it will be a fair day, whereas a dry morning is a sign of rain. This is because the heat absorbed by an object during the previous day will be released as dew or frost (or as condensation on the inside of a car window) when the night and early morning is calm, clear, and cool.

- Rain can be foretold by the phenomenon of far-off shorelines seeming closer than usual. When this happens, rain is usually less than a day away. During fair weather a great deal of salt haze evaporates and is held in the air. The mixing action of unstable prestorm air clears this away, visibility improves, and objects seem closer.

- A halo around the moon or sun is another sign of rain. The halo is caused by the moon shining through the ice crystals of moisture-laden clouds. If the halo is a tight fit, rain is still far off. If the halo forms a large ring, rain is near. If the clouds set in and the moon loses its outline, rain can be expected in about ten hours. The same is also true with the sun.

- When smoke from a ship's funnel curls downward and hangs by the surface, it means rain is approaching. This is caused by the lowering air pressure that precedes rain. Because the air is not dense enough to support the heavier particles in the exhaust, the smoke lingers near the water. Another sign of rain is that a boat's engine exhaust, horn, or any other loud sound, will have a hollow clarity as if heard down a tunnel. This is caused by a lowering of the cloud ceiling so sounds bounce back; in fair weather the clouds are too high to do this.

- Some old sailors insisted that they could smell an oncoming rain storm. This makes sense, because the lowering air pressure allows previously captive odors to escape. Notice how much more ripe seaweed and low tide muck smells before a rain.

You may also notice that if the air is moist and the air pressure already low, that rain will most frequently come at low tide. This is nothing more than the air pressure being further reduced by the lowering of the water's level.

- When the weather is fair, it can be expected to stay that way if the bases of the clouds are high or you see a rainbow to windward. When weather is foul and the wind begins to veer, clear weather is on the way. Wind is said to change its direction by either veering or backing. A wind that veers is changing its direction to your right as you face it. This is a sign of the clockwise rotation of wind that is common to high pressure areas, which bring clear, fair weather. A counterclockwise wind is from an area of low pressure, which brings a promise of foul weather. "A veering wind will clear the sky; a backing wind says storms are nigh."

- All winds have personalities dependent on their direction. Each is surprisingly unique. The west wind, because it travels over land, traditionally brings fair dry weather. This, of course, is not so on the Pacific coast or Gulf coast of Florida where it often brings rain. West winds prevail in the United States and are reversed most often by the presence of an area of low pressure. This brings an east wind with cloudiness, a drop in air pressure, and a rise in humidity.

DEALING WITH THE ELEMENTS

Wind and Storms

On a day-to-day basis the wind is the most important element of weather concerning sea kayakers. Precipitation, while it can be uncomfortable or limit visibility, shouldn't hold you back; and temperature, provided you are well-prepared, should also not keep you off the water (except, of course, in extreme cases). But if you're not careful, the wind will do you in.

Predicting the wind's speed and direction far in advance is very difficult, even for so-called experts. Sailors have been trying with limited success for cen-

turies. So don't knock yourself out doing what can't be done. The one thing you can do is to know what you are dealing with at the moment. Standing on the shore, you should be able to judge what you will be getting yourself into. For every course relative to the wind, and every kayaker's abilities, there are winds that will be too much and winds that will be beneficial. You must be able to judge which you will be facing by sight and by feel.

First, on a global scale, there are prevailing winds that in most of North America travel from west to east.

Land features, both natural and manmade, can affect the winds and how you paddle.

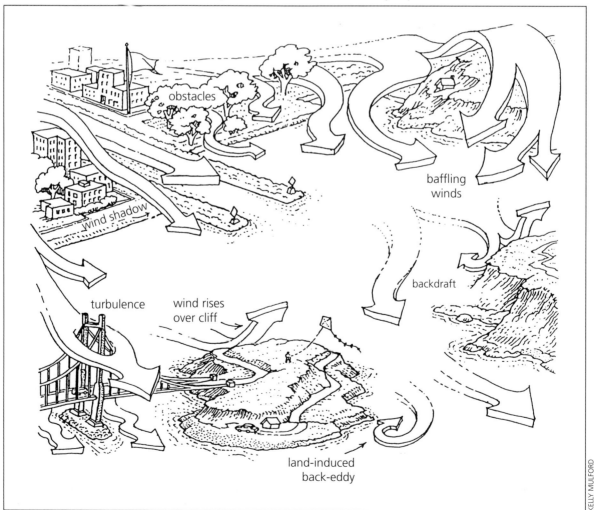

In turn, these are affected by localized winds, such as land and sea breezes. (Incidentally, winds are named for the direction from which they blow: a north wind blows from the north, a land breeze from the land, and a sea breeze from the sea.) As the land heats up during the day, warm air rises and is replaced by cooler air from over the water. This shoreward movement of air, a sea breeze, creeps in around noon, becomes strongest by late afternoon (9–13 knots), then tails off and dies around sunset. Then at night, the land cools and the air above it becomes colder and denser than the air over the water (whose temperature is more stable). This causes a wind from the land toward the water—a land breeze—which starts before midnight and continues until the land is once again heated. Land breezes are seldom more than about 9 knots. Sea breezes can work with or against the prevailing wind, creating stronger winds or canceling them out. Big lakes, such as the Great Lakes, have lake and land breezes that can also work with or against a prevailing wind.

Winds coming off the land will always be more capricious than those that have reached you over open water. Large land features can produce their own wind systems, such as southern California's Santa Ana winds, which are caused by inland desert air tumbling down the coast mountains to the shore. More important to kayakers are the smaller land features that affect the wind: islands cause eddies that whirl around for great distances downwind, and cliffs can cause strong downdrafts.

Some kayakers are interested in determining the wind's speed, either by visual cues or using handheld anemometers. But the only value of knowing the wind's actual speed is in the ability this gives you to understand the increasing forces. The force (in pounds per square foot of pressure) that a wind exerts is exponential to its speed. For example, if the wind doubles in speed from 5 to 10 knots, its force quadruples. A little wind goes a long way, and a little more goes even further.

The most frightening sort of wind for the sea kayaker is anything that comes up fast. At an all-out paddling speed of 6 knots, you're not about to outrun anything. So when the prospect of a line squall or a thunderstorm looms on your horizon, you'd better have a good idea of what it is going to do to leave yourself with the maximum amount of time to take defensive action.

Line squalls form on the edge of a cold front. Whether you're on the bridge of a battleship or in a kayak, it is one of nature's most impressive shows, with the front pushing ahead a boiling, tearing, sulfurous yellow and black cloud with a turbulence that can be heard. As it hits, the wind shifts and comes bowling down at speeds of more than 50 mph. There's thunder, lightning, rain, and a noticeable chill in the air. And then it's over.

Luckily squalls, or any rains associated with a cold front, go as fast as they come, supporting the saying that "the sharper the blast, the sooner it's past." Another lucky point is that they are completely predictable. Any lightning or storm clouds seen in the west or northwest will most likely reach you, but those seen to your south or southeast will pass. If it looks like you are going to get hit, you should prepare yourself for the oncoming winds. Put on rain gear, secure loose items on deck, and get ready to brace. After the clouds go by and a few heavy raindrops fall, the sky may lighten a little, tricking you into thinking that it is over, and then *Wham*! You get blasted by the front itself with heavy rains, lightning, and a cold wind from a new direction. But in a few minutes it's all over; leaving the world and you soaked, shaken, and now bathed in cool, dry air.

Another fearsome yet fast moving terror is the thunderstorm. These can happen on their own, independent of a cold front, created by the upwelling of moist air that has been heated during the day.

Although they can strike at any hour, thunderstorms most often occur in the late afternoon or early evening. Signs to look for are singular, dark cloud formations of great height, terminating in an anvil-shaped top that points in the direction of travel. As with a squall, there is a preceding line of low, rolling clouds. But with thunderstorms, these clouds bring a violent shifting of winds from an updraft, then a brief lull, followed by even more violent downdrafts, lightning, thunder, and rain as the first clouds pass. The downdrafts continue, always blowing out toward the edge of the storm, until the storm has passed over.

Fog

It will happen to you: you'll wake up some morning and the world that was bright and shining the day before will be enshrouded in a dense, dark, slowly swirling mist—you won't even be able to see the other end of the cove. Or you will be paddling, and there, off on the horizon, will be a thin, gray line moving in slowly but surely—fog. As benign as it looks, fog is dangerous to paddlers.

Paddling in fog is not for the inexperienced. Your navigation skills need to be perfect if you are making a crossing rather than hugging the shore. If you are in an area where there is other boat traffic, you will be invisible to larger boats until the crunch of your hull alerts them to a collision.

Assuming you get caught out and cannot wait for fog to clear before you launch—it often lifts in mid-morning, driven away by rising temperatures and breezes—you should make sure a number of safety items are handy: your handheld air horn, flashlight, and charts for navigation. Paddle close to shore where larger boats are unlikely to travel. Groups should stay very close together. It's extremely easy to get separated in a fog, and sound is muffled and confused, so voice contact is limited. For that reason as well, it will be very hard to detect the presence or direction of larger boats. If it is just too difficult to make your way or if your group is getting separated, pull ashore and wait it out. Don't push it in a fog.

Tides

In times not all that distant, it was believed that tides were the respirations of a sea monster. Given the tide's regularity, that's not an inappropriate image. Over most of the world, tides are semidiurnal (twice a day), with two equal highs and lows. The west coast of North America has unequal tides, with one higher high and one lower low. Along the Gulf of Mexico, tides are diurnal (once a day), with only one high and low per day.

Tides are caused by the gravitational pull of the moon, and to a lesser extent (about half), the sun. The result is that the moon, helped or hindered by the sun, drags a bulge of water around the planet with it, with a complementary bulge caused by centrifugal force on the opposite side. The relationship of the sun to the moon affects the tide's range (difference in height), and the time difference between consecutive high and low waters. During a lunar month, the greatest ranges, about 20 percent more than average, occur during spring (as in "rising up")

tides when the sun and moon pull together. The smallest ranges are during neap (from the Old English, "without power of advancing") tides, and are about 20 percent less than average.

Tides and currents are separate entities. Tide is up and down; currents are in and out. The duration of the tidal cycle follows the earth's rotation. Semidiurnal tides change every 6 hours and 12 minutes, producing highs and lows 50 minutes later each day. Tide tables, published for commonly navigated waters, give you information about the tide's range and the time and height of high and low waters to the minute. But local winds (an onshore wind can pile up water in a bay, for example) and weather (a low-pressure area or heavy rains might raise tides) will have their way with these predictions.

Interpreting tide tables is a skill that you may find useful for planning launches or landings, or so you don't get stranded at low tide in a shallow estuary. The heights shown in tide tables do not represent the depth of the water; they are figures to be added to or subtracted from the depths shown on the chart for the area. These charted depths form a plane of reference called the datum line. Charted depths are usually measured at *mean lower low water* (MLLW), the average height of the lowest low tides. So if your chart shows that the beach on which you're camped has a very shallow bay fronting it, and low tide occurs at 7 A.M. the next morning, you had better get up early if you want to have navigable water on which to leave the next day.

Currents

Any movement of water, no matter how slow, will affect your progress in a kayak. But with an understanding of currents, you can turn them into an advantage rather than a hindrance.

Unlike wind, a current's direction, or *set*, is named for the direction toward which it is flowing. The speed of a current is its *drift*, and the time between *flood* (incoming tidal current) and *ebb* (outgoing) when there is no drift is called *slack water*. A tidal current's set, drift, and time of slack water are listed in the government's *Tidal Current Tables*. These tables are accurate, but as with tides, currents can often be affected by wind and weather.

The best current indicators are right there on the water with you. Pilings will have a wave on their up-

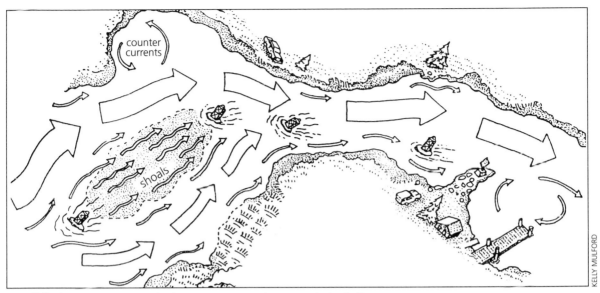

You'll find stronger currents in deeper water, weaker currents in shallow.
Watch for counter currents behind points of land.

current side with a V-shaped wake down-current. Buoys lean with the current. Anchored boats, however, are not reliable indicators, because they swing to the wind as well as the current. The simplest method is to stop your boat's movement through the water and watch reference points on land to see which way you are being set.

If you know the wind's direction, you can also tell the direction of the current. Look at the water's surface. Waves or a chop will form where the current is running against the wind, and the water will be relatively smooth where the wind and current are aligned. Where a strong wind blows against the current, as when an inlet's outgoing tidal stream opposes an onshore wind, a rough sea can result, often making the passage impossible. Look for current lines, usually marked by floating debris, where currents meet. Choose the side you want to be on based on its wind-caused wave pattern.

Learn to use currents to your advantage. They are strongest where the water is deep, and weakest over shallows. On a large lake or the sea, currents (which usually run parallel to the land) are weaker inshore than offshore. Tidal currents change direction along the shore first, with the ebb usually being stronger and lasting longer than the flood. So if you must paddle against a *foul* (on-your-bow) current, stay near shore or over thin water—the current will be weaker and of shorter duration. All currents speed up in restricted passages, and a bend in a channel has its deepest water and strongest currents on the outer curve. Water speeds up around points of land, piers, and such, often with back-eddies on the down-current side.

NAVIGATION

HOW NOT TO GET LOST

There is no great trick to navigating, whether on land or at sea—it's just a matter of knowing where you are. And the trick to knowing where you are is mostly about paying attention to where you've been.

Yes, you'll need to know some techniques and how to use some simple tools. But it still comes down to just paying attention to the world you travel through. Be aware of details, and your chances of getting where you want to go, and back, are pretty good. The "sixth sense" of direction that we hear tales about does exist and is simply the ability to combine this constant awareness with some basic skills.

So before you buy your charts (maps, to a landlubber), compass, and pocket global positioning system (GPS) device and paddle off into the sunset, the first thing you need to do is work on that sixth sense. And to do that you need to hone the other senses, the most important being sight, smell, hearing, and timing. These are the tools that are critical to navigation. You can break a compass, lose a chart, and your GPS can go kaput. But you'll always have at your disposal at least one or more of your natural senses.

A good sense to start with is the ability to judge time relative to distance. Defining a distance as 20 miles can be just as useful as saying it's a seven-hour paddle in calm conditions, but time is sometimes a handier way to express distance, because we all have a natural sense of rhythm. We sense time with an internal pulse, and it is the one "extra" sense that has been substantiated. Humans are just one of many species having a good sense of the passage of time.

Sight is an obvious sense to develop for navigation skills, but don't neglect sounds and smells. Smells, in particular, imprint themselves in our memories. Some people claim that smell is the most acute sense and the last to leave us in death. So open your ears and nose as well as your eyes when observing landmarks along the way.

We all have the ability to remember these details and apply them to finding our way, although some people seem better able to do so than others. One person might remember routes previously traveled by relying on specific landmarks ("paddle past the lighthouse and into the second cove after the large white rock"). But someone else might use a different method, keeping track of how long and in what direction he or she has paddled ("paddle for 30 minutes then turn west").

Neither system is superior, and neither navigator gets lost more often than the other. They're just different ways of navigating, and very often the two methods overlap. An affinity for landmarks might be the reason some navigators have trouble reading charts. Because they respond better to complicated chains of landmarks and not to distances and direction (the defining variables of a chart), they may not feel comfortable using a chart. If this is you, don't worry. Anyone can become an expert chart reader with a little applied effort.

With your well-developed arsenal of natural senses, the next thing you must do is learn to pick out, as you begin any leg of a voyage, an easily identifiable feature that can be used as a reference. This can be a single point, such as a mountain or lighthouse, or a line, such as a coast. If you're making a crossing, you should choose a single point that is always visible to you as you travel. Locate yourself in terms of direction and distance to this reference. Now that you know your starting point, your journey can begin. Your job is to keep track of your reference point and where you are in relation to it. Do this whether you navigate with just your own senses or with a map and compass.

When traveling toward a goal, decide on a route and try to stick to it; if mid-course corrections are necessary, make them deliberate, definite, and retraceable. This way, even if you can't locate your goal, you can retrace your steps to where you started or to interim points along the way. If you just get out there and go for it, you will end up completely confused and lost.

While underway, think of what you and the world around you would look like to a bird overhead. Envision the larger picture and your place in it. This is your mental map. Do this by constantly updating your position through the use of sequential landmarks, or by keeping track of how far and in what directions you have gone. Don't just follow the boats or boat ahead of you. Look around continually.

Try to use your internal rhythm, your natural ability to judge time. Experiments show that many animals can measure time to an accuracy of 0.3 percent. In other words, they would be no more than 3 minutes off after a period of 16 hours, 40 minutes (1,000 minutes). Humans do not have such extraordinary accuracy in judging time. But with practice, we can come to within 10 minutes (although not consistently) in 12 hours—which is good enough in a pinch. Sharpen your rhythm skills by trying to guess the time or how long you have been doing something. By all means take your watch with you, but keep trying to tune in to your innate sense of time.

Problems can arise when our mental maps are influenced by our prejudices, imagination, and unique perceptions. For instance, you might read a guidebook that comments on landmarks or on sights along the way. From the written words, you'll build an image of what you expect to see. But it's not always what you'll find. If you force yourself to be objective, though, you'll probably have to agree that what was written was an accurate description, and that it was you who read something else into it. This is perfectly normal. We concoct images not so much from the way things are, but from the way we think they should be. The two are often very different. Be prepared to revise your preconceptions when they no longer fit your surroundings.

We sometimes have no control over the causes of our getting lost. But there is no excuse for getting lost when it can be prevented.

JONATHAN HANSON

CHARTS AND COMPASSES

Charts

Like a book, a chart is meant to be read, but a chart gives you all its information at once instead of doling it out a page at a time. The trick is to learn how to absorb it in small doses.

The first thing to learn about charts is that they cannot be taken at face value. Charts have been called "truth compressed into symbols," and the symbols need to be interpreted. These paper representations are not exact replicas of the world, and therefore imagination is required to get out what has been put in. Look for significant features within the general pattern of details. Good navigators will plan ahead for alternative routes and landmarks just in case what a chart shows doesn't seem to be there.

Navigational charts carry very little information about the land, usually only the land along the shore, if at all. But they speak volumes about the water and what is under it. They show depths, bottom features, what the bottom is made of, and the positions of navigational aids, such as buoys and lighthouses. The National Ocean Service compiles charts for coastal waters and the Great Lakes. The Army Corps of Engineers covers the navigable inland waterways, lakes, and rivers. Add U.S. Geological Survey (USGS) topographical maps to your chart case if you want information about the terrain above high tide line for day hikes and choosing campsites.

Look for charts at marine supply stores. Always get the most up-to-date chart available. Charts are constantly being revised, so check with the "Local Notice to Mariners" at *www.navcen.uscg.mil*, updated weekly by regional coast guard districts; this gives chart revisions and timely data. To get the chart that shows the most detailed information about your area, choose one with a large scale (1:50,000 to 1:15,000 or larger). Charts with a small scale (1:50,000 to 1:150,000 or smaller) show less detail and offer more generalized coverage of a larger area. Remember: small scale = smaller details over a larger area; large scale = larger details over a small area.

The language of the chart is written in symbols. A few are self-explanatory, but for most you'll need a translating dictionary. The National Imagery and Mapping Agency (NIMA) makes available at its Web site *Chart No. 1*, which explains the colors, numbers, lines, and symbols.

Always compare what is on your chart with what you see. At first what is represented on the chart will look nothing like the world around you, that is, until you learn to see. Start by picking out obvious and known landmarks and finding your position among them. Next, judge distances between the landmarks and then between them and yourself to get a sense of scale. Do the same each time you use a chart for a new area. Finally, don't be afraid to question a chart. Lighthouses fail, shorelines erode, and channels shift in storms. Always use all your navigation skills, not just a chart.

Compasses

Two types of compasses are useful for kayak navigation: a baseplate compass and a magnetic-card compass. You can use both types, sometimes together, sometimes only one.

Before we get any further describing compass types, however, we need to talk a little about north. A compass needle points to what is known as *magnetic north*. Charts are oriented to what is known as *true north,* or *geographic north*. Magnetic north is somewhere to the west of Baffin Island, while geographic north is at the North Pole. In kayak navigation, we are usually only interested in magnetic north.

The difference between geographic north and magnetic north is called *variation* and is measured in degrees and designated either east (E) or west (W). There are places where variation is greater, places where it is less, and places (such as parts of Michigan, Indiana, Ohio, Kentucky, Tennessee, and Florida) where it doesn't exist at all.

Now for compass types. A baseplate compass has a magnetic needle within a dial that rotates on a transparent baseplate. The rotating dial is marked in 2- or 5-degree increments running clockwise. The clear baseplate has north-south orienting lines, as well as an orienting arrow that makes it easy to align the needle with the "N" (north) mark. What makes the baseplate compass so practical is that it gives you a choice of indicating directions either with or without the use of numbered degrees. The base also doubles as a protractor for determining bearings from a chart, and its edges are inscribed with chart scales or a ruler to measure distances. Some com-

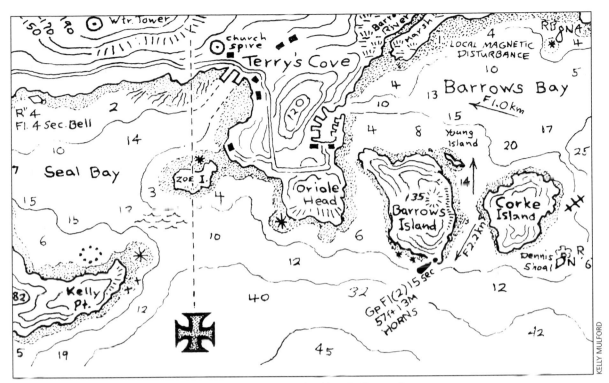

*The cross marks the location of the kayaker, and the dashed line indicates the
kayaker's line of sight on a chart.*

With the line of sight as above, this is what the kayaker actually sees.

passes include an adjustment to compensate for variation, converting magnetic bearings to geographic ones. Other nice, but unnecessary, additions are a magnifier to help read small details and a sighting mirror to help take bearings.

Magnetic-card compasses have the needle and dial joined on a card that rotates as one unit. You should have a magnetic-card compass mounted on the front deck of your kayak, as well as a handheld baseplate compass in your pocket. The advantage of the magnetic-card compass is that "N" on the card is always aligned with magnetic north, so there are no extra steps needed to orient the compass before taking a reading. The disadvantage is that you can't set it to compensate for variation, as you can a baseplate compass. Conversions from magnetic readings to geographic readings, or back, must be done by arithmetic. If all your paddling will be done with a compass alone, and no charts, the magnetic-card type will work quite well. No matter what direction the kayak is pointing the *lubber line*, a mark on the forward part of the case in line with the boat, will show your bearing. All you have to do is mount the compass so you can view the lubber line directly, with the pivot of the compass and the lubber line parallel to the kayak's centerline. This ensures that both compass and boat point in the same direction.

The handheld baseplate compass is used to take a bearing and plot a course with a chart, and the deck compass is used to help you stay on that course. If

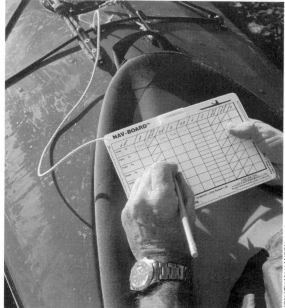

A Nav-Board is a useful tool for recording your direct bearings and back bearings.

you aren't using a chart, use the deck-mounted compass to aid your visual navigation, such as keeping your boat on track to a chosen landmark.

Variation could make plotting a course complicated, but charts are printed with a compass rose, which solves the problem. Each rose has an outer ring aligned to geographic north, and one or two inner rings aligned to magnetic north—with the appropriate variation for your chart's area built in.

A final warning: don't confuse your deck compass by packing anything that is made of ferrous metal under it or in your deck bag.

Compass-Only Navigation

Compass-only navigation is the simple act of picking an object toward which you are going to aim your boat, taking a bearing of that object, and then following that bearing as you paddle. This is called a *direct bearing*.

Taking a direct bearing with your deck-mounted compass is easy. Just point your bow at your target and read the bearing in degrees from the lubber line. You then keep your kayak aligned with this bearing as you paddle.

Taking a direct bearing with your handheld base-

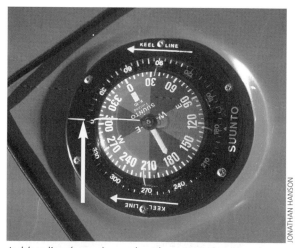

Lubber line (arrow) on a kayak-mounted magnetic-card compass.

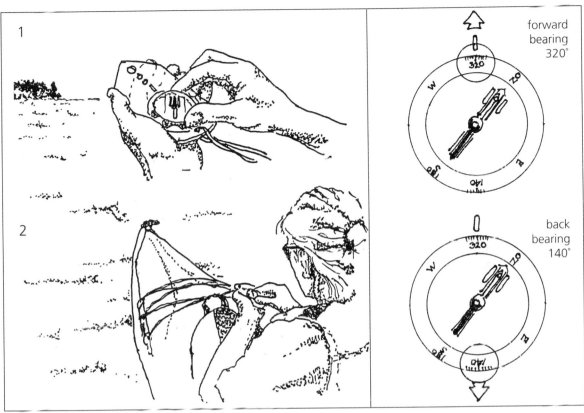

forward
bearing
320°

back
bearing
140°

*Taking a direct bearing: 1. Point compass at object.
2. Turn case until orienting lines on face align with
face needle.*

plate compass is a little more tricky. First, set the
compass to compensate for local variation. Hold it
level at your waist or chest. Point the direction-of-
travel line at the landmark. Turn the case until the
orienting arrow is aligned with the north end of the
needle. Read the bearing where the direction-of-
travel line intersects the case's dial. Careful navigators always use a three-digit notation for bearings,
such as "060 degrees."

Another useful bearing to shoot at the same time
as your direct bearing is a *back bearing*, which is simply 180 degrees opposite your direct bearing. You can
take your back bearing by using a compass or arithmetic. If the direct bearing is 180 or greater, subtract
180 degrees; if the direct bearing is less than 180
degrees, add 180 degrees. Back bearings help to keep
you from being thrown off course by a cross current.

Write down your bearings so that as you paddle
you can refer to them to make sure you're staying

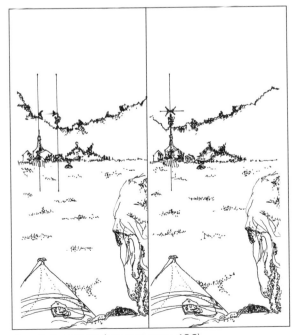

Creating a range (see text page 136).

on track. I often write on the deck with a red grease pencil, which can be rubbed clean later.

With or without a compass, you can help keep yourself on track by lining up two stationary objects along your course. This is called *creating a range*. For example, let's say you line up a steeple and a tall tree. As you paddle, you keep these two objects lined up with each other; if you deviate from your course, the two objects will no longer be aligned.

Navigation with a Chart

Finding a Course from a Chart. On your chart, use a pencil and straightedge to draw a course line from your position to your goal. Then, extend the line through them until it intersects a vertical line such as a line of longitude or a chart border.

Place the baseplate of your compass along the course line and its transparent case over a vertical line. Rotate the case until North and South on the dial (for now, ignore the orienting arrow) are parallel to the vertical line. Read the course at the point at which your course line intersects the dial. Now, hold the compass in front of you and turn your boat until the needle is enclosed within the orienting arrow's outline. Follow that course.

Locating an Observed Object on the Chart. As you're planning your route, sometimes you'll want to locate a faraway object on your chart or a point you can see from the beach or on the water. To do so, mark your position on the chart. Take a bearing of the object you wish to find (step 1 in illustration above right). Place a side of the compass baseplate on your marked position, with the pivot over a geographic north line such as a chart border line or a line of longitude (2). Turn the entire compass by the baseplate until North and South on the dial (not the orienting arrow) are parallel to the geographic north line (3). Your course line (which you marked when you took the bearing) should be pointing toward the object. Draw a line along the baseplate outward toward the object.

Locating Your Position on a Chart. If you don't know where you are, but you can take bearings of identifiable landmarks around you that are on the chart, you can find your position.

First, take back bearings of two or more land-

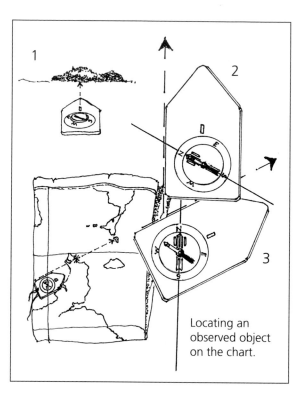

Locating an observed object on the chart.

marks. Ideally the bearing lines from those objects to you should intersect at about 90 degrees; angles of more than 120 degrees or less than 60 degrees will not give you an accurate position. Mark those bearings on the chart using the same method as described for marking a course on a chart, except that when you rotate the case while sighting the bearing, align the orienting arrow with the South (not North) end of the needle. Draw the bearings on the chart by placing the baseplate alongside each object to draw the lines. When the lines are drawn, your position should be reasonably close to where the lines intersect.

GPS Receivers

For less than the price of a good paddle you can now buy a global positioning system (GPS) receiver that will give you your position to within 10–60 feet. A GPS receiver takes continuous readings from a global satellite position-fixing network that can tell you your position by latitude and longitude or Universal Transverse Mercator (UTM) coordinates; speed; direction, distance and time to your destination; how far off course you are; and the path you've taken so you can follow it back or retrace it in the future.

For kayak navigation, the one drawback of a GPS unit is that the information received might not be accurate for a short run. Most units use a pretty short averaging period to compute speed and course; during that time a kayak might not have moved out of the circle of error. Some units allow you to modify the sample time, so be sure to look for this feature. Or you can add a differential beacon receiver, which decodes low-frequency signals sent from U.S. Coast Guard transmitters; these signals boost the accuracy of a GPS unit considerably.

Sound great? Well, it is. But don't throw away your chart and compass. It's still a gadget made of microchips, circuit boards, and wire, and it can go dead without notice, especially on board a wet, bouncy kayak. In addition, satellites can be a little off, or their signals may be affected by atmospheric conditions. Overall, the potential for errors within the GPS system is remarkably low. But if you are depending on this alone, that small probability can become a disaster when it happens. The prudent navigator should never rely on a single source for determining position and will always verify results by other means.

UNDERSTANDING BOAT TRAFFIC

One thing should be clear to you as a kayaker navigating waters with other boats: you are at the bottom of the food chain. You are the smallest and slowest, and invisible to all other boats.

Here are some good, basic survival rules to paddle by.

- Always assume other boats cannot see you.
- Paddle defensively. Wait until you are certain a channel is clear before crossing. Don't try to "race" across the path of an oncoming power boat. Stay out of busy channels and stick to shallow waters where bigger boats can't go. Wear bright colors such as orange, yellow, or white.
- Know the colors of running lights for boats. Red is on the port (left when facing forward) side and green is on the starboard (right).
- If you're not sure that you're out of the way of an oncoming boat, use the rule of "constant relative bearings." When converging with another boat, take frequent compass bearings of that vessel. If the bearings decrease, it will pass in front of you; if the bearings increase, it will pass

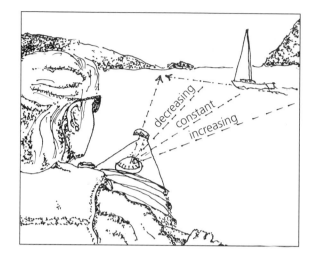

astern. If the bearings remain constant, you are on a collision course and should take immediate action to get out of the way. When you can't take compass bearings, judge the other boat's position relative to the land behind it or by sighting along your hull.

As a defensive kayaker, assume you are invisible to all other boat traffic.

PADDLER'S RESOURCES

FOR DISABLED PADDLERS

A sea kayak is an ideal and almost universal vehicle for those who are willing to try it. For someone confined to a wheelchair a kayak can be a great equalizer. Think of it like this: The human body is not built for nor capable of traveling over the water on its own; in this sense all humans are to some degree handicapped. To overcome this, kayaks were created to sit in while arms are used to move about, just as a person on land uses a wheelchair. This artificial device for transportation on the water, the kayak, is an equalizer.

In sea kayaking a disabled paddler need not be thought of as such; in most cases a disabled paddler is able to participate on a par with able-bodied paddlers. Unlike other sports that have been adapted by the physically disabled as parallel activities, sea kayaking lets you act and be treated as an equal. Because there are more similarities than differences between able-bodied and disabled paddlers, it is your ability, not your disability, that determines with whom you paddle. You are less isolated from the rest of the world and can share experiences with little or no concessions to your handicap. Also, sea kayaking offers its own benefits in that it is highly therapeutic; it builds upper body strength and extends ranges of mobility.

More than the learning process, the biggest challenge of sea kayaking for disabled persons is making the decision to start. Once you get going you'll be pleasantly surprised at how quickly you progress. Set your goals realistically, building slowly to more advanced situations and techniques. Make it as tough or as easy as you like, for you are challenging yourself, not an opponent or anything else, which is what makes sea kayaking so rewarding.

Over the past few years people with special needs have become much more organized. The result has been that opportunities are now available for anyone to lead a more satisfying life with increased access to the world. In the United States, the best place to start is

American Canoe Association Disabled Paddlers Committee, 7432 Alban Station Blvd., Suite B-232, Springfield VA 22150. The committee works with paddlers, would-be paddlers, therapists, and instructors, acting as a clearinghouse for information.

Other organizations are

Challenge Alaska, P.O. Box 110065, Anchorage AK 99511

Environmental Traveling Companions (ETC), Fort Mason Center, Landmark Bldg. C, San Francisco CA 94123

Maui Sea Kayaking, P.O. Box 106, Puunene HI 96784

Nantahala Outdoor Center, U.S. W. Box 41, Bryson City NC 28713

Pacific Water Sports, 16205 Pacific Highway S., Seattle WA 98188

Shared Adventures, Inc., 76 Eastland Ave., Rochester NY 14618

Shared Outdoor Adventure Recreation (SOAR), P.O. Box 14583, Portland OR 97214

Vinland National Center, 3675 Ihduhapi Rd., P.O. Box 308, Loretto MN 55357

Wilderness Inquiry, 1313 5th St. SE, Suite 327 A, Minneapolis MN 55414

Books for disabled paddlers:

Canoeing and Kayaking for Persons with Physical Disabilities: Instruction Manual, American Canoe Association, 7432 Alban Station Blvd., Suite B-232, Springfield VA 22150

Galland, John. Introduction to Kayaking for Persons with Disabilities. Available from Vinland National Center, 3675 Ihduhapi Rd., Box 308, Loretto MN 55357

A Guide to Canoeing with Disabled Persons, British Canoe Union, Mapperley Hall, Lucknow Ave., Nottingham NG3 5FA, England

International Directory of Recreation Oriented Assistive Devices, Life Boat Press, P.O. Box 11782, Marina del Rey CA 90295

Resource Manual on Canoeing for the Disabled, Canadian Recreational Canoeing Association, P.O. Box 398, Merrickville ON, CANADA K0G 1N0

FOR FAMILIES

Kayaks are perfect for families. Of course the word family is an obvious euphemism for kids. So let's just say kayaks are perfect for kids, which they are.

Where to start? Begin with yourself and master the basics. You're going to have to know what you are doing in order to teach your kids. In addition, you have no right risking their safety by not being adequately trained. Also, make sure everyone is dressed properly—top to bottom.

When to start? Probably yesterday. The earlier the better, within reason, that is. Infants make notoriously poor paddlers, but they do enjoy being held or nestled between the legs of a passenger in a triple or, for short distances, by the forward paddler in a double. It's awkward, but it can be done. Your primary worry will be safety. PFDs are available for children down to 20 pounds. Make sure those PFDs have a grab handle on the upper back, flotation in the collar, and leg straps.

The next age group, preschoolers from one to five years, are perhaps the most difficult to deal with. They are too large to hold, too young to paddle, too old to sleep for very long, and they get bored easily. For long trips they may not be the best company because they require an incredible amount of specialized care and gear. At this age they start to become aware of things, which is wonderful; and insist on making some of their own decisions, which can be frustrating. If you hope to get them into kayaking, it is here that you will have to work to make it a fun experience, something they'll look forward to doing again. On a cruise this may not be the easiest thing to do because they are at the height of their "I'm-thirsty-I'm-hungry-I'm-tired-I'm-bored-I-have-to-go-to-the-bathroom" phase. The best pacifier is to go by their schedule, not yours. Keep trips short and add a lot of diversions. If that isn't enough, snack food will usually hold a fidgety kid from insanity (and you from murder) for a while. Patience and seeing things through their eyes is the key to success. A triple-cockpit boat may be your best bet. The center cockpit can be fitted out as a cosy floating playpen with special attention paid to padding and safety. If a triple is not available, a single's rear hatch can be used. This is good only for very short distances because you cannot keep an eye on the child.

You might be better off when they are this age to postpone longer trips and get them started playing in and around kayaks, so there are fewer fears when it comes time for their first lessons. Purposely upset the kayak with all aboard as a game, letting the kids get used to what happens. Give them time to swim and play on and around the boat until it becomes a friendly environment. Make sure they have their own equipment. There's nothing like having a Snoopy PFD with a neat emergency whistle attached to make a kid feel like he or she is part of it, while

also building good safety habits. This is also a good time to enroll kids in swimming classes. A kid in a properly fitting PFD might not need to know how to swim, but being at home in the water could help keep a life-threatening situation from becoming a panicky emergency. Whatever you do, make it fun and don't push it.

Once a child is old enough for grade school, from six years to the early teens, he or she is old enough to try paddling a small kayak solo or paddling along with mom or dad in a double. If you'd like your child to get interested in kayaking, this is the age to do it.

After early adolescence, it may be too late to instill new disciplines. The grip of peer pressure, rebellion, and hyperactive hormones all make it unlikely that you'll have a happy, first-time kayaker on your hands.

By starting kids young, families can be bonded by kayaking. But it must be done carefully. Kayaking is not something the typical kid wants to go out and try. Children have to be introduced to it slowly and in small doses. Two hours is the maximum attention and fidget-free span, so don't just paddle around. Go hide under docks, watch birds, picnic at a nearby beach; whatever you do it must be fun. Once kayaking and fun become synonymous, they'll be hooked and ready for longer trips and more learning.

Put them to work right away. Lack of physical activity gets kids antsy. Let them "paddle" right from the start, but also let them decide when not to. A single-blade paddle if they're in the middle hatch of a triple or a small, double blade if they're forward in a double is best. Get them their own equipment and make sure it's right. A good paddle is just as important for them as it is for you. When you think they're up to it, get them their own boat. A number of companies make kids' kayaks.

Don't underestimate kids' ability to adjust, just give them space, security, and input; you'll be surprised at what they can do. Let them keep lookout and help plan the route. Always let them participate in what's going on. But remember, they are still kids and need their own special support systems. On long trips they'll need their toys, security blankets, teddy bears, books, and your binoculars. Plus, they'll need unusually large amounts of bandages, bug repellent, and toilet paper.

Sometimes it is hard, but parents must not be obsessively goal-oriented when on a cruise with kids. Getting to where you set out for may be your goal but it more than likely is not the kid's. The objective of a kid is to have fun and that means fun in his or her own way. You are going to have to accept the idea of a diversion-centered trip. You've got to go with the flow. Stop and look, picnic and go for a walk, fish, anything to keep it new and interesting. Your challenge is to control the environment while offering progressively more demanding opportunities without over-extending limits of confidence and competence. Think of it as a controlled adventure.

If you are lucky enough to have a kayak-loving teenager, the adolescent years can be the most rewarding. Contemporary teenagers seem to be bombarded with all sorts of unnatural stresses, and sea kayaking can be the perfect escape. For kids who are nonathletic, it lets them get outdoors and taste adventure without having to compete. Kayaking teaches independence, self-esteem, accomplishment, responsibility, and gives something that's just different enough to be interesting without being too "weird." Kayaking is also great for incorporating other interests such as photography, fishing, snorkeling, or a little amateur marine biology.

The bottom line is that sea kayaking is meant to be enjoyed. With some preparation and careful attention to how you approach it, paddling with kids can actually be fun. It can also be rewarding, is definitely inexpensive, frequently is relaxing, almost always brings a family together, and might even make putting up with the occasional "Are we there yet?" worth it.

Books for family paddlers:

Brown, Tom, Jr. *Tom Brown's Field Guide to Nature and Survival for Children*. New York: Berkley Books, 1989.

Logue, Victoria, Frank Logue, and Mark Carroll. *Kids Outdoors: Skills and Knowledge for Outdoor Adventurers*. Camden ME: Ragged Mountain Press, 1996.

GENERAL INFORMATION ON KAYAKING

Periodicals

Atlantic Coastal Kayaker, P.O. Box 520, Ipswich MA 01938; www1.shore.net/~ack/.

Canoe and Kayak, P.O. Box 3146, Kirkland WA 98083; 800-829-3340, 425-827-6363; www.canoekayak.com. Some sea kayaking articles. Best for its annual buyer's guide in December as a comprehensive listing of sources.

Messing About in Boats, 29 Burley St., Wenham MA 01984; 978-774-0906; www.by-the-sea.com/messingaboutinboats/. Frequent sea kayaking articles. Great source for used boats. Published twice a month.

Outside, 400 Market St., Santa Fe NM 87501; 505-989-7100; www.outsidemag.com. Monthly, with a spring annual buyer's guide that's very useful.

Paddler, P.O. Box 775450, Steamboat Springs CO 80477; 970-879-1450; www.paddlermagazine.com.

Paddle Sports, 1509 Seabright Ave., Suite B-1, Santa Cruz CA 95062. All kinds of paddling in all kinds of boats. Published quarterly.

Sea Kayaker, 7001 Seaview Ave. NW, Suite 135, Seattle WA 98107; 206-789-9536; www.seakayakermag.com. The only national magazine dedicated to the sport. Published quarterly.

WaveLength, RR 1, Site 17 C-49, Gabriola Island BC, CANADA V0R 1X0; 250-247-9789; www.wavelengthmagazine.com.

Books

Adney, Edwin Tappan, and Howard Irving Chapelle. *The Bark Canoes and Skin Boats of North America*. Washington DC: Smithsonian Institution, 1964. Development of these craft by Native Americans. Good historical information on Eskimo rolling.

Allyn, Rube. *A Dictionary of Fishes*. 11th ed. St. Petersburg FL: Great Outdoors, 1967. Best field guide for identifying those with whom we share the water.

Anderson, Bob. *Stretching. 20th Anniversary*. Rev. ed. Bolinas CA: Shelter Publications, 2000. Good pre- and post-kayaking exercises

Ashley, Clifford W. *The Ashley Book of Knots*. With amendments by Geoffrey Budsworth. New York: Doubleday, 1993. Over 3,800 knots and their practical usage for everyone from kayakers to tree surgeons. Encyclopedic and practical.

Audubon Society Nature Guides. New York: Knopf, 1985. Guide book series by various authors for the Atlantic and Gulf coasts and the Pacific coast. Animals, plants, and geography of the regions.

Brower, Kenneth. *The Starship and the Canoe*. New York: Holt, Rinehart & Winston, 1978. Multilevel true story about an eccentric Northwest kayak builder and his rocket scientist father.

Burch, David. *Fundamentals of Kayak Navigation*. 3rd ed. Guilford CT: Globe Pequot, 1999. Seat-of-the-pants navigation for those with wet seats. Very complete and practical.

Cassidy, John. *The Klutz Book of Knots: How to Tie the World's 24 Most Useful Hitches, Ties, Wraps, and Knots: A Step-By-Step Manual.* Palo Alto CA: Klutz Press, 1985. Connect-the-dots type instructions for 24 basic knots. Book includes 5 feet of rope.

Chapman, Charles F., and Elbert S. Maloney. *Chapman Piloting, Seamanship, and Boat Handling.* 63rd ed. New York: Hearst Books, 1999. Since 1922, this frequently updated text has been the bible for power and sail boating, with most of the material equally applicable to the sea kayaker.

Craighead, Frank C. *How to Survive on Land or Sea.* 4th ed. Annapolis: Naval Institute Press, 1984. The classic book on survival. Great if that's what you're into, or need.

Daniel, Linda. *Kayak Cookery: A Handbook of Provisions and Recipes.* Seattle: Pacific Search Press, 1986. Camping and cooking for touring sea kayakers.

Diaz, Ralph. *Complete Folding Kayaker.* Camden ME: Ragged Mountain Press, 1994. All you need to know about skin boats and traveling with them.

Dowd, John. *Sea Kayaking: A Manual for Long-Distance Touring.* 4th ed. Seattle: University of Washington Press, 1997. A seasoned kayaker's manual of slightly less esoteric information with a slightly less biased point of view.

Dyson, George. *Baidarka.* Edmonds WA: Alaska Northwest, 1986. History of the Aleut Eskimo, Russian fur traders, and their mutual effect on the local evolution of the kayak and the author.

Eastman, Peter F. *Advanced First Aid Afloat.* John M. Levinson, ed. Centreville MD: Cornell Maritime Press, 2000. Everything from amputations to zits.

Fons, Valerie. *Keep It Moving: Baja by Canoe.* Seattle: Mountaineers, 1986. A 2,400-mile endurance run down the Baja coast. The paddling never stops.

Forgey, William W. *Hypothermia: Death by Exposure.* Merrillville IN: ICS Books, 1985.

Fox, William T. *At the Sea's Edge: An Introduction to Coastal Oceanography for the Amateur Naturalist.* Englewood Cliffs NJ: Prentice-Hall, 1983. An introduction to coastal oceanography for the amateur naturalist and terminally curious.

Gatty, Harold. *Finding Your Way on Land or Sea: Reading Nature's Maps.* Brattleboro VT: South Greene Press, 1983. When everything else fails, there's navigation by observing nature through sight, sound, and smell.

Getchell, Annie, and Dave Getchell Jr. *The Essential Outdoor Gear Manual: Equipment Care, Repair, and Selection.* 2nd ed. Camden ME: Ragged Mountain Press, 2000. A must-have guide for caring for and repairing your outdoor equipment.

Goddard, John. *Kayaks Down the Nile.* Provo UT: Brigham Young University Press, 1979. Down to the sea in folding kayaks,

Groene, Janet. *Cooking on the Go.* New York: Hearst Marine Books, 1987. Three hundred recipes for those with no refrigerator, oven, broiler, grocery store, or Cuisinart.

Halstead, Bruce W. *Dangerous Marine Animals: That Bite, Sting, Shock, or Are Non-Edible.* Centreville MD: Cornell Maritime Press, 1995. How to avoid all those nasty things down there.

Hanson, Jonathan. *Complete Sea Kayak Touring.* Camden ME: Ragged Mountain Press, 1998. How to get started cruising the sea in a kayak, from weekenders to long expeditions.

Herreshoff, L. Francis. *An L. Francis Herreshoff Reader.* Camden ME: International Marine, 1978. Worth it for one chapter, "The Dry Breakers," which tells of a contemplative paddle out to, and night spent on, a barren patch of rocks.

Hutchinson, Derek C. *Derek C. Hutchinson's Guide to Sea Kayaking.* Chester CT: Globe Pequot, 1990. A seasoned kayaker's manual of esoteric information with a biased point of view.

Hutchinson, Derek C. *Eskimo Rolling.* Old Saybrook CT: Globe Pequot, 1999. Everything you ever wanted to know, or thought there was to know, about the subject.

Ilg, Steve. *The Outdoor Athlete: Total Training for Outdoor Performance.* Evergreen CO: Cordillera, 1987. A thoughtful, no-nonsense approach to getting fit that will enhance your sea kayaking experiences.

Kellogg, Zip, ed. *The Whole Paddler's Catalog.* Camden ME: Ragged Mountain Press, 1997. Resources for paddlers, from gear to tools for ocean conservation to paddling music and videos.

Kesselheim, Alan S. *Trail Food: Drying and Cooking Food for Backpackers and Paddlers.* Rev. ed. Camden ME: Ragged Mountain Press, 1998. A handy, carry-along package with everything from pretrip preparation to recipes.

Kissner, J. *Foldboat Holidays*. New York: Greystone, 1940. Interesting period piece about boats in a bag and the paddlers who were beginning to sense their potential.

Lindemann, Hannes. *Alone at Sea*. New York: Random House, 1958. Joshua Slocum's Atlantic crossing in a folding kayak. A great adventure, if not literature.

Makower, Joel, ed. *The Map Catalog: Every Kind of Map and Chart on Earth and Even Some above It*. New York: Random House, 1993. A complete resource for "every kind of map and chart on the earth."

Manley, Atwood, and Paul F. Jamieson. *Rushton and His Times in American Canoeing*. Syracuse NY: Syracuse University Press, 1968. The growth of paddling sports in the United States in the 19th century.

McKie, Ronald. *The Heroes*. New York: Harcourt, Brace, 1961. Desperate escape from the Japanese by Australian commandos in kayaks.

McMenamin, Paul. *The Ultimate Adventure Sourcebook: The Complete Resource for Adventure, Sports, and Travel*. Atlanta: Turner Pub., 1992.

Nansen, Fridtjof. *Eskimo Life*. Trans. William Archer. New York: AMS Press, 1973. Contemporary observations of traditional kayaks, kayaking, and way of life for Greenland Eskimos.

Nickerson, Elinor B. *Kayaks to the Arctic*. Berkeley: Howell-North Books, 1967. One family's story of How We Spent Our Summer Vacation. Theirs was in the Arctic.

Nordby, Will, ed. *Seekers of the Horizon: Sea Kayaking Voyages from around the World*. Chester CT: Globe Pequot, 1989. Excerpts from writings by sea kayakers about their journeys out and, sometimes, back.

Phillipes, Cecil. *Cockleshell Heroes*. London: Heinemann, 1956. British kayak forces behind enemy lines in World War II. Good show!

Putz, George. *Wood and Canvas Kayak Building*. Camden ME: International Marine, 1990. Complete plans on how to build, plus advice on how to use and maintain, a 17-foot and an 18-foot kayak.

Ramwell, J. J. *Sea Touring: An Informative Manual for Sea Canoeists*. Published in 1980 under the aegis of the British Canoe Union, dedicated to producing polished paddlers in a country that insists on calling kayaks "canoes."

Snaith, Skip. *Canoes and Kayaks for the Backyard Builder*. Camden ME: International Marine, 1989.

Tack and tape method of building some good-looking and inexpensive boats from plywood. Plans for a 16-footer and an 18-footer.

Teller, Walter, ed. *On the River: A Variety of Canoe and Small Boat Voyages*. New Brunswick NJ: Rutgers University Press, 1976. Anthology of some of the best writings from the turn of the century about cruising in canoes and kayaks.

United States Coast Guard. *Navigation Rules: International–Inland*, *www.uscg.mil/vtm/pages/rules.htm*. The most recent edition is required reading for those who paddle in populated waters. Rights of way, plus sound, light, and day signals.

Van Dorn, William G. *Oceanography and Seamanship*. 2nd ed. Centreville MD: Cornell Maritime Press, 1993. An encyclopedic work on wind, waves, currents, and how they affect things afloat.

Zimmerly, David W. *Qajaq: Kayaks of Siberia and Alaska*. Juneau: Div. of State Museums, 1986. Readable and beautifully presented historical research into the kayaks of the north Pacific.

Charts and Tide Tables

National Oceanic and Atmospheric Administration, *www.co-ops.nos.noaa.gov/*

National Weather Service, *www.nws.noaa.gov/*

U.S. Coast Guard *www.navcen.uscg.mil*

National Imagery and Mapping Agency, *Chart No. 1*, access from *http://pollux.nss.nima.mil/*

Gatherings

During the course of a year, sea kayakers come together at events such as symposia, festivals, and workshops, for their common benefit. Listed below are only a few of these.

Advanced Coastal Kayaking Workshop. L.L. Bean, Inc., Freeport ME 04033

Alaska Pacific University Kayak Symposium. Alaska Pacific University, 4101 University Dr., Anchorage AK 99508

Angel Island Festival & Regatta. Sea Trek Ocean Kayaking Center, Liberty Ship Way, Sausalito CA 94965

Atlantic Coast Sea Kayaking Symposium. L.L. Bean, Inc., Freeport ME 04033

East Coast Sea Kayaking Symposium. (Charleston SC). TAPS, 12455 N. Wauwatosa Rd., Mequon WI 53097

Great Lakes Kayak Touring Symposium. Great River Outfitters, 3721 Shallow Brook, Bloomfield Hills MI 48013

Hornby Island Kayaker's Festival. Hornby Paddling Partners, RR 1, Hornby Island BC, CANADA V0R 1Z0

Inland Sea Kayaking Symposium. Trek & Trail, P.O. Box 906, Bayfield WI 54814

Jersey Shore Sea Kayaking & Bay Canoeing Show. Ocean County Dept. of Parks, Lakewood NJ 08701

Mystic Sea Kayaking Symposium. Mystic Valley Bikes, 26 Williams Ave., Mystic CT 06355

West Coast Sea Kayaking Symposium. TAPS, 12455 N. Wauwatosa Rd., Mequon WI 53097

West Michigan Coastal Kayaking Symposium. Lumbertown Canoe and Kayak Specialties, 1822 Oak Ave., North Muskegon MI 49445

For more and updated information contact

American Canoe Association, 7432 Alban Station Blvd., Suite B-232, Springfield VA 22150; 703-451-0141; *www.acanet.org.*

Trade Association of Paddle Sports (TAPS), 12455 N. Wauwatosa Rd., Mequon WI 53097; 262-242-5228; *www.gopaddle.org.*

Equipment

The following are not complete lists of all the excellent gear available to North American kayakers. Any omissions are due to lack of space and are not a comment on the quality of any equipment maker.

Kayaks

Alaskan Kayaks, SR-1, Box 2425, Chugiak AK 99567

Aquaterra, P.O. Box 8002, Easley SC 29640

Baldwin Boat Co., RFD 2, Box 268, Orrington ME 04474

Bart Hauthaway, 640 Boston Post Rd., Weston MA 02193

Betsie Bay Kayak, P.O. Box 1706, Frankfort MI 49635

Cal-Tek Engineering, 36 Riverside Dr., Kingston MA 02364

Camp Lake Kayak & Canoe Co., 88 Princess Margaret Blvd., Islington ON, CANADA M9P 2Y9

Current Designs, 10124-G MacDonald Park Rd., Sydney BC, CANADA V8L 3X9

Dagger Kayaks, P.O. Box 1500, Harriman TN 37748

Destiny Kayak Co., 1111 S. Pine St., Tacoma WA 98405

Dirigo Boatworks, Ltd., 616 S. Wichita, Wichita KS 67202

Dragonworks Inc., RFD 1, Box 1186, Bowdoinham ME 04008

Dunn's Custom Built Kayaks, 8991 Gowanda State Rd., Eden NY 14057

Easy Rider Canoe & Kayak Co., P.O. Box 88108, Seattle WA 98138

Eddyline Kayaks, 1344 Ashten Rd., Burlington WA 98233

Feathercraft, 1244 Cartwright St., Granville Island, Vancouver BC, CANADA V6H 3138

Folbot, Inc., P.O. Box 70877, Charleston SC 29415

Georgian Bay Kayak, Ltd., S. S. 1, Site 7, Comp 19, Penetanguishene ON, CANADA L0K 1P0

Gillies Canoes & Kayaks, Margaretville NS, CANADA B0S 1N0

Great River Outfitters, 3721 Shallow Brook, Bloomfield Hills MI 48032

Hydra Kayaks, 5061 S. National Dr., Knoxville TN 37914

Klepper America, 35 Union Square W., New York NY 10003

Loon Kayaks, Box 253, Smallpoint Rd., Sebasco Estates ME 04565

Mariner Kayaks, Inc., 2134 Westlake Ave., Seattle WA 98109

Morley Cedar Canoes, P.O. Box 147, Swan Lake MT 59911

Nautiraid USA, P.O. Box 1305, Brunswick ME 04011

Necky Kayaks, Ltd., 1100 Riverside Rd., Abbotsford BC, CANADA V2S 4N2

Northstar Kayak & Canoe Co., 40 Ayer Rd., Locust Valley NY 11560

Northwest Kayaks, 15145 NE 90th, Redmond WA 98052

P&H Designs, 1107 Station Rd., Unit 1, Bellport NY 11713

Pacific Canoe Base, 2155 Dowler Pl., Victoria BC, CANADA V8T 4H2

Pacific Water Sports, 16205 Pacific Highway S., Seattle WA 98188

Paluski Boats, P.O. Box 147, Grand Island NY 14072

Perception, P.O. Box 8002, Easley SC 29641

Pygmy Kayak Co., P.O. Box 1529, Port Townsend WA 98368

Rainforest Designs/Nimbus, 6-9903 240 St., Albion BC, CANADA V0M 1B0

Rockwood Outfitters, Ltd., 699 Speedvale Ave. W., Guelph ON, CANADA N1K 1E6

Seavivor, 576 Arlington Ave., Des Plaines IL 60616

Seda Products, 926 Coolidge Ave., National City CA 91950

Southern Exposure Sea Kayaks, P.O. Box 4530, Tequesta FL 33469

Superior Kayaks, 213A Dartmouth Ct., Bloomingdale IL 60108

We-no-nah Canoe, Inc., P.O. Box 247, Winona MN 55987

West Side Boat Shop, 7661 Tonawanda Creek Rd., Lockport NY 14094

Wilderness Systems, 1110 Surret Dr., High Point NC 27260

Wind Horse Marine, 91 Library Rd., South Britain CT 06487

Woodstrip Watercraft Co., P.O. Box 1140, Lansdale PA 19446

PFDs

Extrasport, 5305 NW 35th Ct., Miami FL 33142

Lotus Designs, 1060 Old Mars Mill Highway, Weaverville NC 28787

Palm Equipment/Great River Outfitters, 4180 Elizabeth Lake Rd., Waterford MI 48328

Seda, 926 Coolidge Ave., National City CA 91950

Stohlquist, P.O. Box 3059, Buena Vista CA 81211

Paddles

Aqua-Bound, 1-9520 192nd St., Surrey BC, CANADA V4N 3R8

Cricket, 17530 W. Highway 50, Maysville, Salida CO 81201

Eddyline/Swift Paddles, 1344 Ashten Rd., Burlington WA 98233

Lightning Paddles, 22800 S. Unger Rd., Colton OR 97017

Nimbus Paddles, 4915 Chisholm St., Delta BC, CANADA V4K 2K6

Sawyer Paddles, 299 Rogue River Pkwy., Talent OR 97540

Werner Paddles, P.O Box 1139, Sultan WA 98294

Spray Skirts

Kokatat, 5350 Ericson Way, Arcata CA 95521

Palm/Rapidstyle Equipment/Great River Outfitters, 4180 Elizabeth Lake Rd., Waterford MI 48328

Perception, P.O. Box 8002, Easley SC 29641

Snap Dragon Design, 14320 NE 21st St. #15, Bellevue WA 98007

Safety & Navigation Accessories

ACR Electronics (strobes, lights), 5757 Ravenswood Rd., Fort Lauderdale FL 33312

Adventure Medical Kits, P.O. Box 43309, Oakland CA 94624

Atwater Carey (medical kits), 1 Repel Rd., Jackson WI 53037

Great River Outfitters (towing systems, deck pumps), 4180 Elizabeth Lake Rd., Waterford MI 48328

KayakSafe (spray skirt release), P.O. Box 1508, Mill Valley CA 94941

Maptech (NOAA charts on CD-ROM), 665 Portsmouth Ave., Greenland NH 03840

Motorola Sports Radios, 1301 E. Algonquin Rd., Schaumberg IL 60196

See/Rescue (distress banners), 219 Koko Isle Cir., Suite 602, Honolulu HI 96825

Spyderco (knives), 4565 Highway 93, Golden CO 80402

West Marine (radios, flares, distress flags), P.O. Box 50070, Watsonville CA 95077

Clubs and Organizations

For more, and updated, information contact one of the trade associations listed in Gatherings, or see the listings in current paddling magazines.

Alaska

Juneau Kayak Club, P.O. Box 021865, Juneau AK 99802-1865

Arizona

Desert Paddling Association, 620 E. 19th St., Suite 110, Tucson AZ 85719

Southern Arizona Paddling Club, P.O. Box 77185, Tucson AZ 85703

California

California Kayak Friends, Suite A 199, 14252 Culver Dr., Irvine CA 92714

Environmental Traveling Companions (ETC), Ft. Mason Center, Landmark Bldg. C, San Francisco CA 94123

Miramar Beach Kayak Club, 1 Mirada Rd., Half Moon Bay CA 94019

San Diego Kayak Club, 5691 Genoa Dr., San Diego CA 92120

San Diego Paddling Club, 1829 Chalcedony St., San Diego CA 92109

San Francisco Bay Area Sea Kayakers, 229 Courtright Rd., San Rafael CA 94901

Slackwater Yacht Club, B37 Gate 6 Rd., Sausalito CA 94965

Valley Wide Kayak Club, P.O. Box 521, San Jacinto CA 92581

Western Sea Kayakers, P.O. Box 59436, San Jose CA 95159

Colorado

Rocky Mountain Sea Kayak Club, P.O. Box 100643, Denver CO 80210

Connecticut

CONN-YAK, P.O. Box 2006, Branford CT 06405
Nordkapp Owners' Club of America, 47 Argyle Ave., West Hartford CT 06107

Florida

Central Florida Paddle Masters, 2460 Ave. E. SW, Winter Haven FL 33880
Coconut Kayakers, P.O. Box 3646, Tequesta FL 33469
Emerald Coast Paddlers, 7 Bayshore Pt., Valparaiso FL 32580
Florida Sea Kayaking Assoc., 9529 Kuhn Rd., Jacksonville FL 32257
Southwest Florida Paddling Club, 20991 S. Tamiami Trail, Estero FL 33928, e-mail: ERO1@aol.com
Tampa Bay Sea Kayakers, P.O. Box 12263, St. Petersburg FL 33713-2263
West Florida Canoe Club, P.O. Box 17203, Pensacola FL 32522

Hawaii

Hawaii Island Kayak Club, 74-425 Keal a Kehe Pkwy., Kailua-Kana HI 96740
Hui W'a Kaukahi, 732 Kapahulu Ave., Honolulu HI 96816
Kanaka Ikaika Racing Club, P.O. Box 438, Kaneohe HI 96744
Maui Outing Club, P.O. Box 277-330, Kihei, Maui HI 96753

Illinois

Chicago Area Sea Kayakers, 4019 N. Narragansett, Chicago IL 60634
Saukenuk Paddlers' Canoe and Kayak Club, P.O. Box 1038, Moline IL 61265

Louisiana

Bayou Haystackers Canoe and Kayak Club, c/o H. W. Brandl, 8744 Forest Hill, Baton Rouge LA 70809
Gulf Area Open Water Kayaking Assoc., P.O. Box 6743, New Orleans LA 70174-6743

Gulf Coast Open Water Kayaking Assoc., 1640 Harbor Dr., Suite 123, Slidell LA 70458

Maine

Portsmouth Kayak Club, 56 Eliot Rd., Kittery ME 03904
Southern Maine Sea Kayaking Network, P.O. Box 4794, DTS, Portland ME 04112

Maryland

Chesapeake Paddlers' Association, P.O. Box 341, Greenbelt MD 20768
Tantallon International Sea Kayaking Assoc., 12308 Loch Carron Cir., Fort Washington MD 20744

Massachusetts

Boston Sea Kayak Club, 47 Nancy Rd., Newton MA 02167
Cape Ann Rowing and Kayak Club, P.O. Box 1715, Gloucester MA 01931-1715
Martha's Vineyard Oar & Paddle, P.O. Box 840, West Tisbury MA 02575
North Shore Kayakers, P.O. Box 50, Marblehead MA 01945
North Shore Paddlers Network, c/o Daniel Kern, 224 Dearborn Road, Greenland MA 03840
Roofrack Yacht Club, 113 Railroad Ave., Hamilton MA 01982

Michigan

Great Lakes Sea Kayaking Club, 3721 Shallow Brook, Bloomfield Hills MI 48013
International Klepper Society, P.O. Box 973, Good Hart MI 49737
Lansing Oar and Paddle Club, P.O. Box 26254, Lansing MI 48909
Negwegon Kayak Club, 218 West Bay St., East Tawas MI 48703
West Michigan Coastal Kayakers' Assoc., c/o Karl Geisel, 1025 Griswold SE, Grand Rapids MI 49507

Minnesota

Inland Sea Kayakers, 2411 Carter Ave., St. Paul MN 55108
Twin Cities Sea Kayaking Assoc., P.O. Box 581792, Minneapolis MN 55458-1792
Univ. of MN Kayak Club, 108 Kirby Student Ctr, UMD, 10 University Dr., Duluth MN 55812-2496

Upper Midwest Kayak Touring News, P.O. Box 17115, Minneapolis MN 55417-0115

Mississippi

Gulf Area Water Trails Society, Inc., P.O. Box 473, Pearlington MS 39572-0473

Missouri

Great River Paddle Touring Society, 334 S. Marguerite, St. Louis MO 63135

Montana

Flathead Paddlers, 15 18th St. E., Kalispell MT 59901

Ocean & River Kayaking Adventures, 355 Boon Rd., Somers MT 59932

New Jersey

ANorAK, 618 Burke Rd., Jackson NJ 08527

Jersey Shore Sea Kayak Association, 157 Main St., Lebanon NJ 08833

Seabright Paddle Association, c/o Debbie Reeves, 200 Monmouth Ave., Atlantic Highland NJ 07716

South Jersey Sea Kayaker's Assoc., 123 Heathercroft, Egg Harbor Township NJ 08234

New York

Adirondack Mountain Club, Genesee Valley Chapter, 47 Thorpe Crescent, Rochester NY 14616

FLOW Paddlers Club, 4300 Canandaigua Rd., Walworth NY 14568

Huntington Kayak Klub, 51 Central Pkwy., Huntington NY 11743-4308

Metropolitan Assoc. of Sea Kayakers, 195 Prince St. Basement, New York NY 10012

Metropolitan Canoe and Kayak Club, P.O. Box 021868, Brooklyn NY 11202-0040

Sebago Canoe Club, Paerdegat Basin, Paerdegat Ave. N., Brooklyn NY 11236

Touring Kayak Club, 205 Beach St., City Island, Bronx NY 10464

Oregon

Oregon Ocean Paddling Society (OOPS), P.O. Box 69641, Portland OR 97201

Southern Oregon Paddlers, P.O. Box 2111, Bandon OR 97411

Pennsylvania

Pittsburgh Council AYH, 6300 5th Ave., Pittsburgh PA 15232

South Carolina

Low Country Paddle Club, c/o Charlie Mehlinger, 131 Marshland Rd., Hilton Head Island SC 29926

SandLapper Sea Yackers, 525 Longbranch Rd., Gilbert SC 29054

Texas

Houston Canoe Club, P.O. Box 925516, Houston TX 77292-5516

Texas Sea Touring Kayak Club, P.O. Box 27281, Houston TX 77227

Vermont

Champlain Kayak Club, 89 Caroline St., Burlington VT 05401

Virginia

Association of North Atlantic Kayakers, 34 East Queens Way, Hampton VA 23669

Washington

Baidarka Historical Society, P.O. Box 5454, Bellingham WA 98227

Eddyline Paddling Club, 630 Ershig Rd., Bow WA 98232

Lesbian and Gay Sea Kayakers, 1122 E. Pike #896, Seattle WA 98122-3934

Mountaineers, 300 3rd Ave. W., Seattle WA 98119

North Sound Sea Kayaking Association (NSSKA), P.O. Box 1523, Everett WA 98206

Olympic Kayak Club, 22293 Clear Creek Rd. NW, Poulsbo WA 98370

Port Orchard Paddle Club, 2398 Jefferson Ave. SE, Port Orchard WA 98366

Puget Sound Paddle Club, P.O. Box 111892, Tacoma WA 98411-1892

Seattle Sea Kayaking Club, 13906 123rd Ave. NE, Kirkland WA 98034-2247

Washington Kayak Club, P.O. Box 24264, Seattle WA 98124

Whatcom Association of Kayak Enthusiasts (WAKE), P.O. Box 1952, Bellingham WA 98227

Yakima Kayak Club, P.O. Box 11147, Yakima WA 98909

Wisconsin

Mad City Paddlers, 1710 Yahara Place, Madison WI 53703

Peninsula Paddlers, 822 N. 4th Ave., Sturgeon Bay WI 54235, email: rcross@sturbay.k12.wi.us

RASKA, 4805 S. Lakeshore Dr., Racine WI 53403-4127

Schools for Sea Kayaking and Outdoor Skills

This is only a partial listing. For further information, contact one of the sea kayaking trade organizations listed in Gatherings.

Maine Island Kayak Company, 70 Luther St., Peaks Island ME 04108

Monterey Bay Kayaks, 693 Del Monte Ave., Monterey CA 93940

Nantahala Outdoor Center, 13077 Highway 19 W., Bryson City NC 28713

National Outdoor Leadership School (NOLS), 288 Main St., Lander WY 82520

Outward Bound, 945 Pennsylvania St., Denver CO 80203

Southwest Sea Kayaks, 2590 Ingraham St., San Diego CA 92109

Southwind Kayak Center, 17855 Sky Park Circle #A, Irvine CA 92714

Wilderness Medical Associates, RFD 2 Box 890, Bryant Pond ME 04219

Wilderness Medicine Institute, P.O. Box 9, Pitkin CO 81241

INDEX